CarbSmart PRESS

FAT FAST

COOKBOOK **2**

50 More Recipes to Induce Deep Ketosis, Tame Your Appetite, Cause Crazy-Fast Weight Loss, Improve Sports Performance & Generally Improve Your Metabolism

DANA CARPENDER

with Andrew DiMino

CarbSmart Press

A Division of *CarbSmart, Inc.*

http://www.CarbSmart.com

CarbSmart Press
CarbSmart, Inc.

2900 East Patrick Lane, Suite 1
Las Vegas, NV 89120

For information about special discounts on bulk purchases,
please contact CarbSmart, Inc. at customerservice@carbsmart.com.

DISCLOSURE: This document contains links to external websites
that may provide financial benefits to the publisher, the authors,
and/or CarbSmart, Inc. from click-through purchases.

ISBN 978-0-9984417-0-2

Version 1.0

If you have any questions about the content of this cookbook or wish to report any broken links, please email comments@carbsmart.com immediately.

Jonny Bowden, PhD, CNS

aka The Nutrition Myth Buster™, best-selling author of

The Great Cholesterol Myth, The 150 Healthiest Foods on Earth, and Living Low Carb

"No one knows more about whipping up easy and delicious low carb dishes than Dana Carpender. It's easy to see why she's the guru of the low-carb cooking world. Read this terrific cookbook and you'll instantly become a fan!"

Ellen Davis, MS

Ketogenic-Diet-Resource.com, Author of Fight Cancer with a Ketogenic Diet

"Many years ago, Dana's work was instrumental in helping me go low-carb and regain my health. I now recommend all of Dana's books to my readers. They are fun to read and informative, and her new Fat Fast Cookbook 2 is another winner. If you are looking to jump-start your weight loss, or just get back into ketosis and feel better quickly, this book will help."

Martina Slajerova

KetoDietApp.com, Author of The KetoDiet Cookbook and Sweet and Savory Fat Bombs

"Dana has created a fantastic resource for anyone following a healthy low-carb diet. With over 50 delicious recipes, including quick snacks, comfort meals and guilt-free desserts, the new Fat Fast Cookbook has you covered. Whether you are interested in the fat fasting technique or simply follow the ketogenic diet, this book is a must have!"

Dedication

This cookbook is dedicated to every low-carber that struggles with their low-carb lifestyle like I do. We struggle not because the lifestyle is difficult or unattainable, we struggle because of all the damage we did to our metabolisms over the years because we listened to the "experts" that told us to eat a low-fat, calorie restricted diet for all those years.

It is also dedicated to my girlfriend Margie who supports my efforts to make our lives better as we help those in the community who also need help.

Andrew S. DiMino
Publisher, President, and Founder
CarbSmart, Inc.

Also From *CarbSmart*

FAT FAST
COOKBOOK

by Dana Carpender, Amy Dungan, & Rebecca Latham

Jump-Start Your Low-Carb Weight Loss
with CarbSmart's Fat Fast Cookbook

Are you having trouble losing weight, even on the Atkins Induction phase?

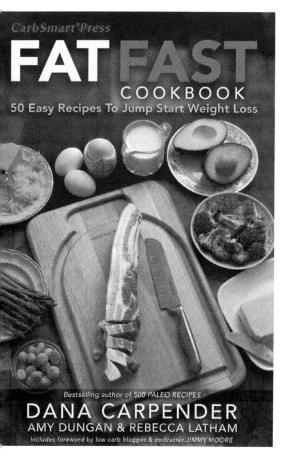

Have you lost weight successfully on low-carb, but hit a plateau or started to regain weight even though you're still following your low-carb diet?

Are you looking for a way to add more healthy fat to your low-carb diet?

Are you interested in jump-starting your weight loss the low-carb way?

The Fat Fast Cookbook contains 50 easy Low-Carb / High-Fat recipes to jump start your weight loss or get you into nutritional ketosis, using the Fat Fast as developed by Dr. Atkins in his history-changing book Dr. Atkins' New Diet Revolution.

GRAIN-FREE
SUGAR-FREE LIVING COOKBOOK

by Dana Carpender & Caitlin Weeks, NC

50 Amazing Low-Carb & Gluten-Free Recipes For Your Healthy Ketogenic Lifestyle

"The legendary Dana Carpender does it again, this time in company with Paleo nutritionist and fitness expert Caitlin Weeks. A collection of simple and straightforward recipes, this book is perfect for the sugar-free, grain-free newbie. Think going low-carb or Paleo means

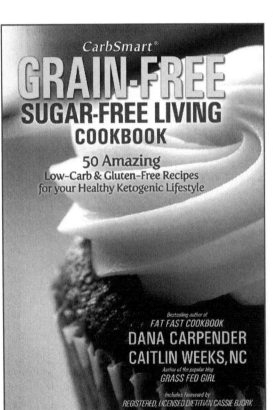

you will have to miss out on sweet treats and delicious baked goods? Dana and Caitlin turn that idea on its head. Enjoy everything from muffins and cookies to your favorite coffee house drinks, all without those pesky sugars and grains. They also include tips on grain-free baking and cooking, as well as how to source the necessary ingredients. Healthy living and clean eating start here."

*—Carolyn Ketchum, Writer and Photographer
All Day I Dream About Food,
alldayidreamaboutfood.com*

CarbSmart

LOW-CARB & GLUTEN-FREE

Holiday Entertaining

by Tracey Rollison & Misty Humphrey

90 Crowd-Pleasing Low Carb, Gluten Free Recipes for Entertaining a Few or a Whole Houseful for the Holidays

Are you tired of hosting holiday parties that leave you unable to eat any of the food you've made for your guests? Suffer no more. With CarbSmart Low-Carb & Gluten-Free Entertaining by your side, you'll finally be able to host the holiday parties of your dreams and eat everything you serve. The best part? Even your gluten- and carb-loving guests will shower you with compliments. Holiday entertaining has finally been made healthy.

EASY GLUTEN-FREE ENTERTAINING

by Christine Seelye-King & Aimee DuFresne

50 Delicious Gluten-Free Party Recipes For Every Occasion

Whether you're hosting a small intimate gathering of friends or a large party with an open guest list, Easy Gluten-Free Entertaining will satisfy everyone whether they live gluten-free or not.

Inside you'll be treated to practically limitless gluten-free recipe and menu ideas safe for anyone eliminating wheat or gluten from their daily lives. Not only are all these recipes gluten-free, most of them are also grain-free, nut-free, dairy-free, vegetarian, and/or vegan.

Your next social gathering will be a success because the recipes included make it easy to satisfy any and all palates and preferences whether your guests follow a gluten-free lifestyle or not. From delicious appetizers to main dishes, side dishes, and dessert look no further than Easy Gluten-Free Entertaining.

Contents

Get Social with CarbSmart

facebook.com/CarbSmart

twitter.com/CarbSmart

yummly.com/page/carbsmart

pinterest.com/CarbSmart

youtube.com/c/CarbSmart

google.com/+CarbSmart

instagram.com/CarbSmart

Foreword

By Jacqueline A. Eberstein, R.N.

Dana Carpender is well known in the low carb community for her prolific collection of low carb recipes that can make our lifestyle more fun and interesting. I personally appreciate that many of her recipes are quick and easy.

This book can fill a gap by expanding choices for those who use or want to use the Fat Fast originated by Dr. Robert Atkins. A review of the Fat Fast can be found in *What is the Fat Fast and Why Do We Do It?* on page 15. Dr. Atkins used the Fat Fast for those patients who could not break a plateau or who were unable to develop any degree of sustained ketosis.

In recent years there has been an increased interest in the use of a variety of fasting techniques, although fasting has a history going back thousands of years. It has been used for health reasons, for religious observances, for weight loss, to stimulate fat burning, for cleansing and detox and even for protesting or making political statements. There is also great interest in using various forms of calorie restriction to increase longevity.

Utilizing the Fat Fast or other methods of fasting stimulates the body to switch from glucose burning to fat oxidation to supply energy. When carbohydrates are kept low (below about 50-60 grams daily) and protein moderate, healthy metabolic changes occur. Importantly, blood sugar and insulin levels are lowered, allowing access to fat stores for energy. Utilizing fatty acids from triglycerides (stored fat) creates ketones (beta-hydroxybutyrate) in the blood, nature's backup fuel. This is called nutritional ketosis.

Despite many experts telling us we must consume 130 grams of carbohydrates per day to fuel the brain, The Institute of Medicine states that there is no minimal dietary intake of carbohydrates needed. Ketones can easily and more efficiently meet our fuel needs including fueling the brain. The few tissues in the body that are glucose dependent have their needs easily met by *gluconeogenesis* (the manufacture of glucose from protein or fat in the liver).

If you want to Fat Fast but are concerned about ketones, it is important to clarify that nutritional ketosis is safe and effective. It is confused with diabetic ketoacidosis, a condition that only occurs in people who are insulin deficient with uncontrolled high blood sugar levels. Ketosis has been greatly misunderstood even by trained medical personnel. Within hours of birth, newborns are in ketosis. Our hunter-gatherer ancestors depended on ketones to give them the energy to hunt when fasting.

The safety of ketosis from carbohydrate restriction has been known for a long time. Dr. Richard Veech, a researcher working for the National Institutes of Health has studied ketosis for decades. He states "Doctors are scared of ketosis. They're always worried about diabetic ketoacidosis. But ketosis is a normal physiological state. I would argue that it is the normal state of man." He further states that ketones are "magic" and has shown that both the heart and brain are 25% more efficient on ketones than glucose.

The benefits derived from the Fat Fast and ketosis are many. For those wanting to lose weight comfortably, ketones decrease hunger and ease cravings. The state of ketosis has positive effects on the brain. One of the earliest uses of a ketogenic diet was to control seizures. Now an easier-to-use modified version of an Atkins diet is often used for intractable seizures, especially for kids. Ketones are also being studied to address other severe neurological conditions such as Parkinson's, Alzheimer's, ALS, brain cancer and others. Benefits may be derived because ketones provide such a steady and efficient energy source. Additionally, when carbs are low enough to access fat stores, blood sugar and insulin levels stay healthier, avoiding the damage that high levels of insulin and glucose cause. Medical conditions such as diabetes, polycystic ovary syndrome and increased inflammation—related to most chronic disease including cancers and cardiovascular disease—can be improved.

This is just a small sampling of the reasons creating and keeping a good level of ketones in the blood is so important completely apart from weight issues. The Fat Fast and Dana's creativity offer the opportunity to take advantage of this vehicle to enhance not just your external appearance but your general health as well.

References:

1. Taubes, G. What if it's All Been a Big Fat Lie? New York Times, 2002

   https://www.fatfastrecipes.com/cookbook-104

2. Veech, Richard L., et. al. Ketone Bodies, Potential Therapeutic Uses, 2001

   https://www.fatfastrecipes.com/cookbook-105

What is the **FAT FAST** and Why Do We Do It?

by Dana Carpender

This section is reprinted from the original Fat Fast Cookbook for those people who have not read it yet. There are minor edits to reference recipes in this cookbook.

Everything You Know Is Wrong

For decades we have been told that fat makes us fat. After all, the logic goes, since fats have nine calories per gram, while proteins and carbs have four calories per gram, if we slash the fat from our diets, we'll be able to eat the same or an even greater volume of food and lose weight. After all, a calorie is a calorie is a calorie. Right?

WRONG. Prepare to have your mind blown.

What is a Fat Fast?

A Fat Fast is a diet in which a) caloric intake (joules, if you're in that part of the world) is strictly limited, and b) the vast majority of those calories—ideally 90%—come from fat. In <u>Dr. Atkins' New Diet Revolution</u>, Dr. Robert C. Atkins recommended using a Fat Fast of 1,000 calories per day, 90% of them from fat, to break through metabolic resistance to weight loss.

What kind of crazy idea is that?!

A really brilliant crazy idea, and one backed up by research.

For over 30 years, we have been told that all that matters is calories-in versus calories-out; if we wish to lose weight, limiting calories is all that matters, not where those calories come from. That's why we have *100 calorie packs* and ads for everything from yogurt to breakfast cereal to soup that tout, not how nutritious they are, but how few calories they contain. But is the calorie theory correct?

There's little doubt that most people will lose weight if they restrict calories sufficiently, regardless of the source of those calories. If you ate just 200 calories per day of Moon Pies, you would very likely lose weight. Also your energy, your health, your muscle mass, and possibly your hair. But hey, you'd lose weight.

But will you lose an equal amount of weight with the same degree of caloric restriction, regardless of the source? Will the same percentage of pounds lost come from your stored fat mass, rather than your lean body mass? Or does the kind of calories you eat make a difference in how much fat you burn?

I assume that you've guessed by now that it does, or I wouldn't be writing this. How big a difference? A really, really big difference. Dig this:

In 1956, a groundbreaking study appeared in the highly respected medical journal The Lancet. Two British researchers, Prof. Alan Kekwick and Dr. Gaston L. S. Pawan, decided to look at this question of whether the type of calories consumed affected fat burning. A few years earlier, Dr. Alfred Pennington published an article in the Journal of Clinical Nutrition regarding his experience treating obesity with a calorically unrestricted ketogenic diet. Pennington asserted that his patients did not experience the drop in basal metabolic rate that usually accompanies caloric restriction, because *ketosis* allowed them to access their stored body fat, giving them all the energy—the calories—they needed to maintain the higher metabolic rate. (Ketosis is a physiological state where, because you're not feeding it glucose—carbs—your body is running on fatty acids (fat burning, yay!), and a by-product of fat burning called *ketone bodies*, or ketones for short. Most of your body's tissues can run on fatty acids, but some, especially the brain, cannot, but can burn ketones just fine.) Kekwick and Pawan wanted to expand on this information.

Here's what they did: They put obese subjects on low-calorie, *balanced diets*, at levels of 2,000, 1,500, 1,000, or 500 calories per day. Each patient stayed on each version of the diet for seven to nine days. You will be unsurprised to know that the fewer calories they ate, the more weight they lost.

Next, Kekwick and Pawan put obese subjects on one of four different diets. The diets all had the same calorie count—1,000 calories per day—but the *composition of those calories* varied: 1,000 calories of a mixed or balanced diet, 1,000 calories with 90% from carbohydrate, 1,000 calories with 90% from protein, or 1,000 calories with 90% from fat. If it were true that a calorie is a calorie is a calorie, then patients should have lost roughly the same amount of weight on all four diets. Did they?

No. Indeed, on the high-carbohydrate diet the patients actually *gained* a little weight, overall—on just 1,000 calories per day. They lost some weight on 1,000 calories per day of a balanced diet, and even more on 1,000 calories per day with 90% from protein. But overwhelmingly, patients lost the most weight on 1,000 calories per day when 90% of those calories came from fat. Kekwick and Pawan concluded, *So different were the rates of*

weight-loss on these isocaloric diets that the composition of the diet appeared to outweigh in importance the intake of calories.

Finally, Kekwick and Pawan determined that a group of patients could maintain their weight on 2,000 calories per day of a mixed or *balanced* diet. Then they put them on a diet of protein and fat, but very little carbohydrate. They found that their patients could consistently lose weight on 2,600 calories per day so long as carbohydrate was sharply restricted. This was one of the early pieces of research establishing a standard low-carb, Atkins-style diet for long term weight loss and maintenance.

In the 1960s, Dr. Frederick Benoit, working at Oakland Naval Hospital, put seven obese men on a total fast for ten days. They lost an average of 21 pounds each, which sounds great—but it turned out that 14 of those pounds were lean body mass. The subjects were losing far more muscle than fat. Bad ju-ju. Benoit then put the same men on 1,000 calories per day, with 90% of those calories from fat. If a calorie really is a calorie, they should have lost less weight, and certainly less fat, than they did eating nothing at all.

But they didn't. They lost less weight, yes—an average of 14 pounds in ten days. But only 0.5 pounds of that weight, on average, came from lean body mass. Benoit's subjects had lost *nearly twice as much fat* eating 1,000 calories per day as they had eating nothing at all—and they'd protected their muscle mass in the process.

I trust the potential is clear.

How I Got Interested In This

As I write this, I have been eating a low-carbohydrate diet for 17 years (for this second cookbook, it is now 21 years)—more than 30% of my life. It has been hugely beneficial to me, and helped me go from a size 20 to a size 12. However, like so many low-carbers, I reached a plateau—my weight was staying off, but I was still a little bigger than I wanted to be.

I had read about Fat Fasting in Dr. Atkins' New Diet Revolution, and had also seen the work of Kekwick and Pawan, Benoit, and Pennington. It had been in the back of my mind that I needed to try it sometime, I just hadn't gotten around to it.

Suddenly I needed to drop ten pounds, fast, before shooting a television pilot. I tried the Fat Fast, lost a pound a day, felt fine doing it—even had a great weight-lifting workout—and improved my blood sugar readings in the bargain. I was sold.

It's funny how ideas seem to reach a critical mass, and suddenly take hold. In the past year, several friends of mine, long-time low-carbers, have tried eating a higher percentage of fat, with excellent results. It seems that the time has come.

What About All That Fat? And Cholesterol! Won't It Kill Me?

In a word: No.

First of all, if you've been eating the Standard American Diet, you won't actually be getting much more fat than you are already eating. The average American gets 45% of his or her calories from fat. If you're eating around 2,000 calories per day—a not-unlikely number—then cutting back to 1,000 calories per day, 90% from fat, will result in your eating exactly as much fat as you've been eating all along. You're not increasing fat. You're just cutting out the other stuff.

If you've been eating an Atkins-style low-carb diet all along, you may well eat less total fat on a Fat Fast, for the simple reason that you'll be eating less, period.

Some of you are thinking, *Shouldn't I eat healthful fats?* Yes, you should—but you may be thinking of the wrong fats. Animal fats are just fine on a Fat Fast—and in general—and so are butter, cream, and cream cheese. It's polyunsaturated vegetable oils, like soy oil and safflower oil, that you must avoid, along with hydrogenated vegetable oils, aka *trans fats.*

Secondly, the whole *saturated-fat-causes-heart-disease* hypothesis has been largely discredited. According to the World Health Organization in 2010, *Intake of SFA [saturated fatty acids] was not significantly associated with CHD (coronary heart disease) mortality... SFA intake was not significantly associated with CHD events (e.g., heart attacks).* In the same year, <u>The American Journal of Clinical Nutrition</u> published a meta-analysis of 21 studies that looked at the effects of saturated fat consumption on coronary artery disease. The conclusion?

A meta-analysis of prospective epidemiologic studies showed that there is no significant evidence for concluding that dietary saturated fat is associated with an increased risk of CHD or CVD (coronary vascular disease).

A Great, Big, Huge Caution: DO NOT IGNORE

If you are a diabetic and taking any form of blood-sugar-lowering medication, especially insulin, DO NOT UNDERTAKE a Fat Fast WITHOUT MEDICAL SUPERVISION. Why? Because your blood sugar will drop so fast, your medication will need drastic adjustment within 24 hours or less. Your dosages of insulin and other hypoglycemic medications are predicated on your usual intake of carbohydrate. If you suddenly stop eating carbs, those dosages will be way, way too high.

<u>Dr. Eric Westman</u>, one of the country's premier researchers into low-carbohydrate nutrition, has worked extensively with diabetics. He cuts their insulin and other hypoglycemic medications in half on Day One of eating 20 grams per day or fewer of carbohydrate. They

are told to monitor their blood sugar very closely, and medication is adjusted accordingly. Just about everyone has to reduce medication over time, and most need no medication at all if obesity was the cause of the diabetes.

However, you DO NOT WANT TO DO THIS UNSUPERVISED. Insulin shock can be fatal. Do not screw around.

We (the publisher, the authors, and CarbSmart, Inc.) recommend you find a doctor who is hip to carbohydrate restriction for diabetes control, and get on a standard low-carb diet— Atkins, Protein Power, or the like—with that doctor's help. Read Dr. Bernstein's Diabetes Solution and the Atkins Diabetes Revolution to get a handle on the situation. Once your body has adjusted to carbohydrate restriction and your doctor has adjusted your medication accordingly, then you can consider trying a Fat Fast if you're not losing weight, or if you hit a plateau—but we still recommend you have a doctor's supervision.

This caution applies to anyone on blood-sugar-lowering meds for any reason, by the way— for instance, for polycystic ovarian syndrome (PCOS) or non-alcoholic fatty liver disease— and also to those who have been diagnosed as seriously hypoglycemic.

A Far Less Dire Caution

We are assuming that most people reading this are already on a low carbohydrate diet. If, instead, you have been eating American Standard (full of junk), or a low fat/high carbohydrate diet, whether of processed food or whole grains and beans, you have trained your body to run on glucose rather than fat. That can be changed, but it takes a transition period. Your body takes a few days to a few weeks to get with the program and create the enzymes necessary to burn fat for fuel instead of glucose. Because of this, going straight to a Fat Fast from a diet rich in carbohydrate will very likely make you feel awful for a few days—your body simply won't know where to get energy. We very much recommend that you go on a standard low carbohydrate diet first—we're big fans of The New Atkins For a New You, Dr. Atkins' New Diet Revolution, and Protein Power. Any of these very similar plans will give you an easier transition than jumping straight to the Fat Fast. Indeed, you may well find they're all you need to lose weight and improve your health.

Isn't Ketosis Dangerous?

No.

The confusion about ketosis comes because Type 1 diabetics have to be careful about *ketoacidosis*. Wikipedia (Some scoff at Wikipedia, but it's been shown to be on a par with the Encyclopedia Britannica for accuracy, and it's updated far more often) defines **keto*acidosis*** as a *pathological metabolic state marked by extreme and uncontrolled*

ketosis. This causes extremely high ketone levels, combined with very high blood sugar and acid accumulating in the blood. Again from Wikipedia, *In healthy individuals this normally does not occur because the pancreas produces insulin in response to rising ketone/blood glucose concentration.* In other words, this doesn't happen simply from carbohydrate restriction. If you have a functioning pancreas, you can't go into runaway ketosis. If you're making more ketones than your body is happy with, it will convert a little protein to glucose, release a little insulin, and bring your ketone levels down a bit.

The Benefits of Nutritional Ketosis

Dietary ketosis or nutritional ketosis appears to have numerous benefits. In particular, it provides energy while sparing muscle tissue. This would have been vital for our hunter-gatherer ancestors, who might well have to go out to hunt and gather on an empty stomach. In our modern age, ketogenic diets have long been used to treat epilepsy, and are now showing promise for <u>treating cancer</u> and <u>Alzheimer's</u>. And despite years of dire warnings about kidney damage, <u>recent mouse studies show a ketogenic diet reversing diabetic kidney damage</u>.

(There is a modestly increased rate of kidney stones among children on a severely limited ketogenic diet for seizure control. This apparently happens because liquids are restricted to allow ketones to build up in the blood. Liberalizing fluids generally solves the problem. So drink plenty of fluids.)

Here's what <u>The Journal of the International Society of Sports Nutrition</u> has to say about ketones:

During very low carbohydrate intake, the regulated and controlled production of ketone bodies causes a harmless physiological state known as dietary ketosis. Ketone bodies flow from the liver to extra-hepatic tissues (e.g., brain) for use as a fuel; this spares glucose metabolism via a mechanism similar to the sparing of glucose by oxidation of fatty acids as an alternative fuel. In comparison with glucose, the ketone bodies are actually a very good respiratory fuel. **Indeed, there is no clear requirement for dietary carbohydrates for human adults. Interestingly, the effects of ketone body metabolism suggest that mild ketosis may offer therapeutic potential in a variety of different common and rare disease states.** *(Emphasis mine.)*

Dr. Lubert Stryer, Professor of Biochemistry at Stanford University and the author of a <u>biochemistry textbook</u> used in many medical schools, says ketones are, *normal fuels of respiration and are quantitatively important as sources of energy.* (In this usage, respiration doesn't mean breathing, but rather cellular respiration, the basic processes involved in creating energy within the cells.) *Indeed, heart muscle, and the renal cortex [kidney] use [ketones] in preference to glucose.*

Another biochemistry text, this one by <u>Drs. Donald and Judith Voet</u>, says that ketones *serve as important metabolic fuels for many peripheral tissues, particularly heart and skeletal muscle.*

Ketogenic diets similar to the Fat Fast, only without caloric restriction, have been used successfully for decades to treat epilepsy, and a 2006 article in the journal <u>Behavioral Pharmacology</u> states, *there is evidence from uncontrolled clinical trials and studies in animal models that the ketogenic diet can provide symptomatic and disease-modifying activity in a broad range of neurodegenerative disorders including Alzheimer's disease and Parkinson's disease, and may also be protective in traumatic brain injury and stroke.* (The same article includes the information that *The ketogenic diet may also protect against various forms of cell death.)*

Sounds encouraging to me.

Because cancer cells are glucose-dependent, ketogenic diets are also being studied for cancer treatment.

Finally, here's the <u>abstract</u> from an article titled *Ketogenic diets: additional benefits to the weight loss and unfounded secondary effects:*

It is also necessary to emphasize that as well as the weight loss, ketogenic diets are healthier because they promote a non-atherogenic lipid profile, lower blood pressure and diminish resistance to insulin with an improvement in blood levels of glucose and insulin. Such diets also have antineoplastic (anti-cancer) benefits, do not alter renal or liver functions, do not produce metabolic acidosis by Ketosis, have many neurological benefits in the central nervous system, do not produce osteoporosis and could increase the performance in aerobic sports.

Ketones are your friend.

Fat Fast Game Rules

Let's cut to the chase: How to do this?

I'll be honest: Because fat is very high calorie, 1,000 calories per day, 90% of them from fat, is not a lot of food. You won't be eating meals. Instead, you'll be having four to five small *feedings* per day, about two to four hours apart—a cup of coffee with heavy cream for breakfast, an ounce of macadamia nuts three hours later, then in a few hours, a bowl of buttered shirataki noodles, and a couple of hours after that, perhaps a serving of low-carbohydrate vegetables in a high-fat sauce.

Here are the game rules:

Aim for 1,000 calories per day, with 90% of those calories coming from fat. Do not exceed 1,200 calories per day, or eat less than 80% of calories from fat.

Divide those calories among four to five *feedings* per day, each of about 200 to 250 calories. Space these out so that you're eating a little something every three to four hours.

Other than the high-fat, portion-controlled beverage recipes in this book—which count as *feedings*—drink zero-calorie beverages: water, tea, coffee, sparkling water. I cannot recommend that you consume much diet soda; there's too much evidence that it can stall weight loss and make you hungry.

If you eat something a bit low in fat, deliberately make up for it with something quite high in fat at your next feeding.

I regret to tell you that alcohol is right out. Sorry. You might try some of the relaxant herbal teas on the market; your local health food store should have a selection.

Take a good, strong multi-vitamin every day. You should be doing this anyway.

Keep track. There are good nutrition-counter apps available inexpensively, though they're likely to encourage you to eat low-fat. Ignore that part, just track your calorie count and percentages. Online, FitDay.com has a free nutrition tracker program I've used to good effect. I also have the free Calorie Counter & Diet Tracker app by MyFitnessPal on my iPhone. The problem with these apps is you'll need to enter ingredients one by one.

At the very least, keep track of your calories. If you balance the lower fat feedings with higher fat ones, the fat percentage should take care of itself.

Can You Give Me a Sample Menu?

Menu isn't really the right word, since it suggests more than one dish at a time. You won't be doing that on a Fat Fast. You'll be eating only a handful of nuts, or a cup of coffee with cream, or a couple of stuffed mushrooms, or a salad—just one food—at a time. You'll then wait a few hours, until actual, physical hunger sets in, and eat another dish.

I've tried to make this day's menu work-day friendly—you can assemble all the ingredients for the Salted Caramel Mocha Keto Coffee on page 90, except for the coffee itself, in the blender before bed, and set your coffee maker to brew just before your alarm goes off. This means you can pour the hot coffee in the blender, run it for a minute, pour it into a car cup, and be out the door—and even skip the line at the local coffee place.

Likewise, I've chosen two recipes, the Parmesan Stuffed Mushrooms on page 63 and the Celery Salad on page 92, that can be made ahead and that travel well. Have each in a snap-top container in the refrigerator, ready to grab and go. The mushrooms will need a microwave, but most workplaces provide those these days. The Saganaki on page 64 and the Spaghetti with Bacon and Olives on page 78 are for your after work feedings.

Feel free to simplify, though. If you like, double the coffee recipe and take the second serving to work in a Thermos, then snack on ¼ cup of pecans or walnuts in the afternoon. It's all good.

A daily menu might look like this:

7 am: **Salted Caramel Mocha Keto Coffee**
on page 90
(236 Calories, 26g Fat, 91.7% fat)

10 am: **Parmesan Stuffed Mushrooms**
on page 63
(224 Calories, 21g Fat, 82.9% fat)

1 pm: **Celery Salad**
on page 92
(202 Calories, 22g Fat, 95.6% fat)

4 pm: **Saganaki**
on page 64
(212 Calories, 21g Fat, 83.7% fat)

7 pm: **Spaghetti with Bacon and Olives**
on page 78
(203 Calories, 19g Fat, 85.5% fat)

1077 calories, roughly 88% of them from fat. (I got that percentage by adding up the percentages of each recipe and dividing by 5. I understand that's not completely accurate, but honestly, it's the best I can do. That's why I said "roughly.")

But Won't I Be Starving?

Very likely not. Within a day or two, Fat Fasting will induce a state of deep nutritional ketosis—in other words, your body will shift from running on glucose (sugar) to running on fat and ketones. The vast majority of the tissues in your body can run happily on fat and ketones, especially your brain. If you've been eating a low-carb diet, you should have no hitch. If you've never slashed carbs before, you may have a day or two of feeling tired and groggy until your body remembers how to run on the fat/ketone fuel mix instead of on the glucose you've been feeding it. (However, if you haven't tried a low-carb diet, really, good old Atkins is the place to start, rather

than this fairly radical protocol. Read <u>Dr. Atkins' New Diet Revolution</u> or <u>The New Atkins for a New You</u>, and get going!)

Here's the cool thing: Ketones have a profound appetite-suppressant effect. You may be mildly hungry the first day or two, but after that you should be fine. Just space your feedings out, eating only when you feel physically hungry.

I'm not uncomfortably hungry when I Fat Fast. Harder, is getting over the tendency to eat just to eat—grab a handful of something as I'm walking through the kitchen, or sit down to dinner because the clock says it's time. Most of us eat unconsciously, and there's no room for that on a Fat Fast. After a day or two, though, I'm so un-hungry that even this doesn't bother me much.

The Hardest Part

Honestly, the hardest part of Fat Fasting is getting up to 90% of calories per day from fat. Unless you like to eat straight butter, or can afford to eat nothing but macadamia nuts, it's hard. It's also hard to hit that 1,000 calorie mark exactly.

I have found that so long as I stay above 80% calories from fat, and under 1,200 calories per day, I lose weight like crazy, and am in a deep, appetite-suppressing ketosis. I'm guessing those numbers will work for you, too. After all, Kekwick and Pawan and Benoit's subjects had a dietary ward's kitchen making and measuring all their food for them. We're doing this at home, and are unlikely to be quite so precise. Shoot for the 90% fat/1,000 calorie mark, but if you find you've gotten to, say, 84% fat and 1,142 calories, no harm, no foul.

Dr. Atkins recommended a Fat Fast of five feedings per day, each with 200 calories. I find that unnecessarily rigid. The recipes in this book are designed to have 200 to 250 calories per serving—a few a little higher or lower—with 80% or more of those calories from fat. If you choose a recipe with 80% fat, balance it with higher fat feedings during the same day.

Unlike most cookbooks, this one is not arranged with a beverage chapter, an appetizer chapter, salads, soups, etc. Instead, I have grouped the recipes by fat content. This makes it easier to shoot for that 85 to 90% mark. If you have a recipe from the first chapter early in the day, have one from the last chapter later on. Conversely, if you have, say, <u>Salted Caramel Mocha Keto Coffee</u> on page 90, at 92% fat, for breakfast, you can afford to have one of the lower-fat dishes later on.

Portion Control Is Essential

Remember that Fat Fasting isn't just about eating a very high-fat diet, it's also about caloric restriction. Because fat is so high in calories, it is easy to blow past the caloric limit. So long as you are Fat Fasting for quick weight loss, you should strictly observe the portions listed in the recipes. Many of the recipes make only one serving, so you don't have to worry about dividing a recipe into equal portions. Others make multiple servings. You'll need to be scrupulously honest with yourself when dividing them up.

If you've purchased this book because you're maintaining deep nutritional ketosis for sports performance, long-term weight loss, or therapeutic reasons, and want ideas for increasing your fat intake, portion control becomes less important.

Fiber and Water

Because a Fat Fast is calorie-restricted, and because fat is high in calories, portions can be quite small. For example, a portion of macadamia nuts is just ¼ cup. I find those nuts will keep me sated for a few hours, but they're not a satisfyingly big portion if I really feel like a meal.

If you crave a good-sized portion of food on a Fat Fast, your two best friends are fiber and water. Because they have neither usable calories nor carbs, these two items are *free*, or darned close to it. Add fat, and you get a dish that derives the vast majority of its calories from fat.

What foods can you use this way? Broth is mostly water, so soups made from broth plus fat, generally heavy cream or <u>full-fat canned coconut milk</u>, are good choices. Similarly, you'll find some high-fat coffee drinks in this book.

Very low-carb vegetables are largely a combination of fiber and water; add olive oil to make a salad, or butter, <u>coconut oil</u>, or other fat to sauté. <u>Shirataki noodles</u>, too, are pretty much a fiber-and-water blend, and can be used to make a satisfying portion. When I'm really hungry, I'll make a Fat Fast cream soup and serve it as a sauce over shirataki noodles.

Keep fat and water in mind as you create your own Fat Fast recipes.

More About Fiber

I've had a few queries from people wondering how they can get enough fiber on a Fat Fast. Using the fiber-and-water strategy will help. If you like, you can also take a sugar-free fiber supplement, but I really don't think you will need to. First of all, I'm unconvinced that fiber, in and of itself, has a nutritional benefit. I think its good reputation comes from the fact that fiber-conscious folks tend to eat more vegetables and less junk food in general than people who aren't paying attention. Too, since fiber displaces some digestible carbohydrate, it can lower the diet's blood sugar impact. On a very low-carbohydrate diet, this is not a concern.

As for what we politely call *regularity*, it's unlikely to be a problem. All that fat greases the skids. But you can take a sugar-free fiber supplement if you really feel the need.

Long Term Strategy

One trusts that you're not going to try to eat 1,000 calories per day, 90% from fat, forever. It is, as you may suspect, very restrictive. Furthermore, it's not enough protein for the long run.

However, Fat Fasting is a great strategy for losing five to ten pounds very quickly, and for jump-starting stalled weight loss. Dr. Atkins recommended that a Fat Fast last only three to five days. I've done it for eight days with no apparent ill effect. And as mentioned earlier, Dr. Benoit fat-fasted his subjects for ten days. I can't recommend taking it further than that.

Remember, we're not talking only about eating a very high-fat diet, we're also talking severe caloric restriction. It's the caloric restriction that is not appropriate for long-term use. After all, if you're eating only 1,000 calories per day, 900 of them from fat, that leaves only 100 calories for protein and carbs combined. Since protein runs four calories per gram, you can only get a maximum of 25 grams of protein per day on your Fat Fast, and that's if you eat no carbs at all, which is unlikely. Such a low protein intake is fine for the short run—as Benoit demonstrated, fat-fasting spares muscle mass—but it's insufficient for long-term use.

I asked <u>Jacqueline A. Eberstein, RN</u>, who was Dr. Atkins' right hand for thirty years, about his recommendation that people only Fat Fast very short term. She said that Dr. Atkins' concern was that people would abuse the Fat Fast, using it for quick weight loss, but never making the transition to a long-term low-carbohydrate diet. Using the Fat Fast sporadically, while eating a high-carb diet in between times, could lead, Atkins felt, to weight cycling, and eventually metabolic syndrome. Please, don't do this.

How to transition to a long-term strategy?

Here's my experience: For many years my low carb diet averaged around 1,800 to 2,200 calories per day, with somewhere around 100 to 120 grams of protein. Sadly, as I've aged, my body has gotten better at *gluconeogenesis*—converting protein to glucose. Though my blood sugar generally was normal, I started running pre-diabetic fasting blood sugar first thing in the morning. My doctor told me my liver was creating sugar from protein while I slept. He put me on metformin and Victoza, two blood-sugar-lowering medications. Even so, my morning sugar often ran in the 100 to 110 range.

Then I tried Fat Fasting. Very rapidly, my fasting blood sugar was running a tad too low—as low as 69 one morning. I dropped the Victoza—it was expensive and involved sticking myself with a needle.

After a week of Fat Fasting, I went to an every-other-day Fat Fast for several weeks, eating my usual low-carb fare on alternate days. My blood sugar got better and better, and I eventually dropped the metformin, too.

I have not continued with the every-other-day Fat Fast—I had a <u>cookbook to write</u>—but I have permanently reduced my protein intake to 70 to 80 grams per day, and increased my fat. Most days, I don't keep track of calories, but when I do, I find I'm getting more than 80% of my calories from fat. (Unless I drink alcohol, which skews the percentages.)

My blood sugar is not just normal, but considerably better than it was when I was on medication. When I had blood work done this past summer, my HbA1C (a measure of blood sugar over the previous three months) had dropped by 0.4 points as compared to last year—from 5.1 to 4.7 (that 5.1 indicated my blood sugar was normal overall, despite the high fasting sugar, but 4.7 is better).

Super-star blogger and podcaster, Jimmy Moore, has also reduced protein and increased fat, with the result that he has, at this writing, lost 60 pounds, and is crowing about his dramatic increase in energy.

If you've been low-carbing for a while and have plateaued at a higher weight than you'd hoped, or you still aren't getting the blood sugar levels you and your doctor want, you need to consider reducing protein intake permanently. Half a gram for every pound of body weight is about right (a gram per kilo if you live in the civilized world), with very little carbohydrate, and the rest of your calories coming from fat. These recipes will help.

Jackie Eberstein tells me that my every-other-day Fat Fast strategy was actually not a good idea, because it takes the body longer than that to really shift metabolism. Jackie is smarter, more educated, and far more experienced with the ins and outs of low carbohydrate nutrition than I. I will not try every-other-day Fat Fasting again, and cannot recommend it.

Instead, consider using the Fat Fast to break stalls, or if, despite a low-carbohydrate diet, your weight creeps up a few pounds. You might include a three to five day Fat Fast monthly or quarterly.

Jackie also says that in her current practice, <u>Controlled Carbohydrate Nutrition</u>, she often puts people on the Fat Fast five days per week, with an Atkins Induction Diet on the weekends. She says many people find this easier than Fat Fasting straight through.

Other Uses For These Recipes

These recipes are valuable for anyone who wants to be in nutritional ketosis.

Ketogenic diets have been used for decades to <u>control seizures in children</u>. I hope these

recipes help epileptic children and their parents find more variety and interest in what can be a very restrictive diet.

Because cancer cells rely on glucose, there is growing interest in <u>ketogenic diets for cancer patients</u>.

Researchers Jeff Volek and Steve Phinney, in their groundbreaking book, <u>The Art and Science of Low Carbohydrate Performance</u>, have made a strong case for a ketogenic diet for athletes. Because it allows athletes to easily tap into stored fat for energy, instead of relying on limited stores of glycogen, a ketogenic diet has tremendous benefits, especially for endurance athletes.

Ketogenic diets also show promise for <u>preventing and treating Alzheimer's disease</u>. Since Alzheimer's has been tied to elevated blood sugar, and even dubbed type 3 diabetes, this is not surprising. Brains with Alzheimer's cannot properly use glucose for fuel, but can still run on ketones. Having watched helplessly as my mother disappeared into the twilight world of dementia, I find the reports that ketogenic diets are improving and even reversing Alzheimer's exciting beyond all telling.

I hope the recipes in this book will be useful for folks in all these groups.

The Fat Fast Is It For You?

by Jacqueline A. Eberstein, R.N.

This section is reprinted from the original article written for CarbSmart.com and is included for those people who have not read it yet.

During my 30 years working with Dr. Robert Atkins, one of the most difficult issues to address was helping patients who seemed to be doing everything right, yet found weight loss extremely difficult. We considered those patients metabolically resistant to weight loss. It was as if their bodies had lost the key to opening their fat cells to utilize their fat stores for energy.

Why does this happen? I don't have a definitive answer, but in my experience it is more common in women, especially when hormones are changing. Additionally, many prescription drugs cause weight gain, or make it harder to lose. It can also be the result of reaching a set point, and seems to be more common after frequent weight cycling.

We used many methods to help these patients: a 20-gram-per-day carbohydrate restriction to normalize high insulin levels, evaluation and treatment of thyroid, identification of yeast and food intolerances, all circumstances that inhibit weight loss. Yet there were still patients that needed more drastic solutions.

What is the Fat Fast?

Back in the 1970s, when Dr. Atkins was writing his first book (<u>Dr. Atkins' Diet Revolution</u>), he found research done by <u>Drs. Kekwick and Pawan in the '50s and '60s</u> that demonstrated little weight loss on a 1,000 calorie per day diet consisting mostly of carbs. However, weight was lost on a diet of 1,000 calories per day of mostly fat and a little protein. Of course, with more fat and almost no carbs in the diet, people who are ketone resistant usually began to produce ketones.

Cutting calories is an effective strategy for dealing with severe metabolic resistance. The Fat Fast is a 1,000 calorie per day diet, with about 90% of those calories from fat, eaten in five 200 calorie feedings spaced throughout the day.

As a test, follow the Fat Fast plan for five days. Most people are able to do this.

Weigh yourself the first morning of the Fat Fast. Then on the sixth morning, record your weight loss. If you were able to follow the plan, cycle on five days and off two days. Follow a strict Induction plan on the 2 days of no more than 20 grams of carbohydrate per day, but without the strict caloric limitation. I recommend that the 2 days off be on the weekend to allow more food flexibility. However, that's your choice. Continue to weigh as described above and record your progress.

Most people can follow this plan, although the first two days or so can be difficult. Hunger should be reduced by the third day. If hunger remains an issue, increase to 1,200 calories daily in 5 feedings.

It is possible to lose weight on the Fat Fast, then regain a bit on the two days of Induction. But the end result should be a downward pattern, helping you break that set point. Once you have lost enough weight you should be able to resume Induction full-time and continue losing. Keep in mind that the Fat Fast is not meant to be a long-term solution.

The Fat Fast is not for you if

- You lose weight easily. Atkins is a lifestyle designed to personalize carb intake from weight loss to lifetime maintenance. A low calorie diet like the Fat Fast is not appropriate for a quick fix. A very rapid and excessive weight loss can be dangerous to some people due to loss of minerals.

- You are just beginning Atkins. It should be used only after following Atkins as described in one of the many books available. One should not begin with the Fat Fast or resort to it without troubleshooting other causes of slow weight loss. Most people do not need to use the Fat Fast if they follow Atkins correctly.

- You have a week when you don't lose any weight. The scale doesn't change nice and evenly week in and week out. It would be wonderful if it did. Inch loss is a much better indicator of fat loss. Most people will continue to lose inches even if the scale doesn't move regularly. Just have patience.

Try the Fat Fast as a last resort if you can't break a plateau (no weight or inch loss for 4 weeks).

ATKINS CENTER FOOD CHOICES ON THE FAT FAST

Choose any 5 of the following items and space during the day. Items may be repeated on the same day.

1 ounce macadamia, Brazil or walnuts—about 15 nuts.

2 ounces cream cheese, St. Andre cheese, brie or other full-fat cheese.

2½ ounces beef.

3 slices slab bacon.

2 hard boiled egg yolks with 1 ounce of mayo or mixed with ½ a California avocado.

2 ounces of sour cream mixed with 1 tablespoon caviar. Serve with 3 or 4 pork rinds.

2 hard-boiled egg yolks with 2 tablespoons mayonnaise (or try Dana's Fat Fast Ketonnaise recipe on page 82). Serve with 3 or 4 pork rinds.

2 ounces chicken, egg, shrimp, salmon, ham or crab mixed with 1½ tablespoons mayonnaise.

1 ounce chicken, egg, shrimp, salmon, ham or crab with 1 teaspoon mayonnaise with ½ California avocado.

2 ounces heavy whipping cream, sweetened with no carb syrup. You can beat to make a fluffy mousse.

Like all phases of Atkins even the Fat Fast can be individualized while keeping the fats high as you slowly increase calories. Some people can move up to 1,200 calories with 300 calories at 4 meals daily.

Be sure to follow Dr. Atkins recommendation to take an iron free (unless you are iron deficient) multivitamin/mineral. This was a standard recommendation for all of his patients.

Stay hydrated.

As you're in the process of losing be sure to educate yourself on the phases of Atkins to enable you to find your maintenance level that can last for a lifetime. If you have been a weight cycler in the past, know that you can learn to maintain a healthy weight forever.

Fat Fast Carrier Foods and Stretchers

by Dana Carpender

If you like, you can Fat Fast by eating very small portions of very high fat foods—macadamias, pecans, or walnuts, cream cheese, or heck, even olive oil shooters. This approach has the benefit of saving on both time and cooking. But if, like me, you're a born cook, the idea of living like this for longer than a day or two may not appeal to you.

Or, perhaps, you simply want a larger portion, something that consists of more than a few mouthfuls. After all, eating is fun—even during a Fat Fast.

Enter what I call "carriers"—very low carb and low calorie ingredients that carry the fat along with them. You might also call them "stretchers," since these ingredients stretch the size of your portion without wasting the calories.

Basic Fat Fast Carrier Foods and Stretchers

What's low carb and low calorie? Water. Good ol' water. Nobody ever got fat drinking water. Of course, you don't have to use plain water, although I often thin <u>full-fat canned coconut milk</u> with water. You can use broth, especially good homemade bone broth, coffee, diet soda, club soda and/or sparkling water, or even one of the popular "water enhancers." If you simply drink ten cups of coffee per day, each with two tablespoons of heavy cream, you will be on-plan, albeit probably a little twitchy. You can also add cream or coconut milk to diet soda for an ice cream soda knock-off, or to broth for a creamy soup. (Melting cream cheese into broth also works well.)

Fiber, too, creates volume—indeed, it's sometimes referred to as "bulk"—without jacking up the usable carb or calorie contents. You can, of course, combine the two.

More Fat Fast Carrier Foods and Fillers

There are other combinations of water and fiber, of course. We call them vegetables. All of the very low carb vegetables are great for this purpose.

For example: 2 cups of romaine lettuce tossed with 1½ tablespoons olive oil and 2 teaspoons vinegar (plus a little salt and pepper and perhaps a pinch of dry mustard) will have 196 calories, 90% of them from fat. 3 grams of carbohydrate, 2 of 'em from fiber. Better than just drinking olive oil, no?

2 ounces sliced mushrooms sautéed in 1 tablespoon of butter, with 1 tablespoon heavy cream and 1 tablespoon crumbled bleu cheese stirred in to make a sauce, will have 197 calories, 87% of them from fat. This is somewhat more interesting than eating the butter, cream, and bleu cheese without the mushrooms.

The lowest carb vegetables include everything leafy—lettuce, spinach, greens, cabbage, arugala, you name it. Zucchini and summer squash are quite low, as are asparagus, celery, and cucumbers. Oh, and radishes! Broccoli and cauliflower work, too.

Mushrooms (Go with the common button mushroom, cremini, or portobello. Beyond that, look 'em up. I was startled by the carb content of shiitake mushrooms.) and eggplant are both low carb, and have an added virtue: They absorb fat. I often use mushrooms to absorb and hold fat in a recipe—see the recipe for Dana's Fat Fast Chili on pp 51. Stuff a mushroom with a good, rich filling and bake it, and the mushroom will obligingly reserve most of the melted fat for you.

Eggplant's sponge-like capacity to absorb olive oil is legendary. (Truly. Look up the story behind the famous Turkish dish "Imam Bayildi", or "The Imam Fainted.") If you're a fan, feel free to sauté a slice of eggplant in 2 tablespoons of olive oil, with a touch of garlic. I didn't include it, though, because you really could only have one slice at a "feeding," and I hate to leave you with all that leftover eggplant.

If you're improvising with very low carb vegetables—a fine idea—consider roughly 2 ounces to be a serving.

You get the gist: You can mix your fat freely with carb- and calorie-free liquids, and with somewhat more care with foods that combine water and fiber, but have very few usable carbs.

Shirataki Noodles
– the Fat Faster's Best Friend

by Dana Carpender

Enter shirataki noodles. For those of you who haven't discovered them yet, shirataki noodles are traditional Japanese noodles consisting virtually entirely of fiber and water. They have almost no carbs nor calories. Yet they expand your teeny Fat Fast feedings to satisfying proportions. The more times I do a Fat Fast, the more shirataki I eat.

Shirataki are made from glucomannan, a fiber derived from the konjac or konyaku root. Apparently Japanese food manufacturers have seized upon "yam" as the English word for "root vegetable." Hence, often shirataki are labeled "yam noodles," and you may well see "yam" in the ingredient list. Fear not; they are not carby like sweet potatoes.

There are two basic kinds of shirataki: Traditional and tofu. Traditional shirataki are made from only glucomannan fiber. They are translucent and sort of gelatinous, very different from the noodles you grew up with. I really only like them in Asian-style dishes like sesame noodles or pho. The most popular brand of traditional shirataki is Miracle Noodles but other popular brands include NOoddles and Skinny Noodles.

Tofu shirataki by House Foods, as the name suggests, have a little bit of tofu added to the glucomannan fiber. This makes them white. It also makes them somewhat more tender than the traditional variety. The texture is not identical to that of Western-style pasta, but I enjoy tofu shirataki in all sorts of applications, from macaroni and cheese to pasta salads. If you,

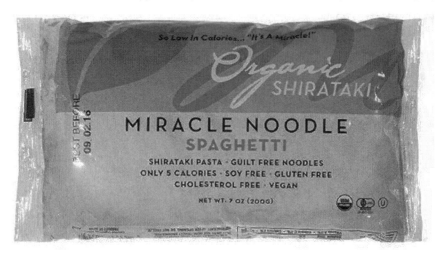

like many, avoid soy, be aware that, so far as I can calculate, tofu shirataki contain perhaps a couple of teaspoons of tofu per packet. I don't eat much soy, but I don't fret about tofu shirataki.

Nasoya brand also makes shirataki with a little potato starch and chickpea flour instead of tofu. I prefer the ones with tofu, but know people who choose the Nasoya soy-free shirataki. You might try them both.

New to the game are shirataki noodles made with konjac flour and oat fiber (a water soluble fiber). This new version of shirataki noodles provides a texture and look that more closely resembles the familiar, Western-style pasta and noodles. Leading this product category is Better Than Foods in pasta, noodles and rice versions.

Shirataki come in a variety of shapes. I stock tofu shirataki in spaghetti, fettuccini, and macaroni shapes; there is also angel hair. (For quite a while I had to special order the macaroni shirataki through my health food store, buying a case at a time. Apparently they decided other people would like them, too; they've started stocking them along with the other shapes.)

As I said, I only like the traditional shirataki noodles in Asian-style dishes, so I only buy them now and then. But I have discovered a new form of shirataki: Miracle Noodle Miracle Rice. Traditional shirataki in small pellets about the size and shape of short-grain rice, Miracle Rice has been a welcome addition to my kitchen. (Wait until you try my Fat Fast Fried "Rice!" on page 67)

Preparing Shirataki Noodles

Shirataki noodles come prehydrated in a pouch of liquid. This throws some people off. The liquid smells fishy; some people never get past it. Too, without proper preparation shirataki will ooze water into your dish, diluting your sauce and leading to disappointment, perhaps even cursing.

Here is the best method I have found for preparing shirataki:

This method works for all shapes and styles including Miracle Rice. Put a strainer in your sink. Snip open the pouch and dump in your shirataki. Yes, the liquid smells like fish. Panic not. Rinse your shirataki well. If you're using one of the long, skinny shapes you might also snip across them a few times with your kitchen shears. They tend to be long to the point of unwieldiness.

Dump your rinsed shirataki into a microwaveable bowl and nuke 'em on high for two minutes. Drain them again—yes, back into the strainer. Back into the bowl, and nuke for *another* two minutes. Drain them one more time. Your shirataki are now ready for use. Mostly I put them right back in the same bowl and go from there.

Basic Fat Fast Shirataki Noodles Recipe

You'll find many recipes for shirataki noodles in this book. As I said, the more I do the Fat Fast, the more shirataki I eat. But if you'd like something super quick and easy, add 1½ tablespoons of butter, 1 tablespoon of whipped cream cheese, 1 tablespoon grated Parmesan, and maybe a teeny sprinkle of garlic powder. Nuke 'em for another 30-45 seconds, stir 'em up, and they're done. 210 calories, 94% of them from fat. How perfect is that?

I like House Foods brand tofu shirataki, and the most well known rice-shaped shirataki is Miracle Rice. But the selection of shirataki burgeons; you may find a brand you like better.

Shirataki Noodle Brands

- House Foods Tofu Shirataki
- Miracle Noodle
- NOoodles
- Better Than Foods
- Konjac Foods

Shirataki keep for at least six months in the refrigerator, and I haven't found that a week or three at room temperature (in the sealed pouch, of course) does them any harm. Feel free to stock up. However, be aware that freezing turns shirataki into mush.

Please note that some online retailers ship shirataki noodles unrefrigerated or at room temperature even during the summer. When we used to sell them at CarbSmart.com, we did this all the time and never had any go bad in transit.

About Low-Carb Sweeteners

by Dana Carpender

The Sweetener Wars are the bane of my existence. No matter what sweetener I use in a recipe, someone will complain. "How can you use sucralose? It's artificial!" "Stevia tastes nasty, and it's so expensive. Why don't you use Splenda?" "I can't stand the cooling sensation from erythritol!" Etc, etc, etc.

My solution is to write recipes with the sweeteners I find most suitable for getting the flavor and nutritional breakdown I want, but to tell you how to substitute other sweeteners if you like.

Liquid Stevia

You must know the sweetness equivalence of the sweetener you choose. I have often used liquid stevia in various flavors in this book. I use both Sweetleaf and NOW Better Stevia brands of liquid stevia. They are about equally sweet, taking about 6 drops to equal a teaspoon of sugar in sweetness and 18 drops to equal a tablespoon of sugar in sweetness. While inexact, I

find that using ¼ teaspoon of either of these brands of stevia is roughly equivalent to ¼ cup of sugar, ½ teaspoon is equivalent to ½ cup of sugar, etc.

6 drops of NOW Better Stevia or Sweetleaf liquid stevia to equal a teaspoon of sugar in sweetness

18 drops of NOW Better Stevia or Sweetleaf liquid stevia to equal a tablespoon of sugar in sweetness

¼ teaspoon of either of these brands of stevia is roughly equivalent to ¼ cup of sugar, ½ teaspoon to ½ cup of sugar

Liquid Flavored Stevia

If you replace liquid flavored stevia, you'll need to compensate not only for the sweetness, but also for the flavor chosen—add a little vanilla, chocolate, or lemon extract, depending on the flavor of stevia desired. I've also used English toffee stevia. **LorAnn** makes English toffee flavoring, available at craft stores that carry fancy cake-baking supplies or, like everything else, through Amazon.com.

Sugar-Free Coffee Flavoring Syrups

You can also use sugar-free coffee flavoring syrups, which come in many flavors, including vanilla, chocolate, English toffee, and caramel. While there are a few brands available, and I have tried and liked them all, DaVinci Gourmet syrup company was the only one to respond to my request for information. They tell me that their sugar-free syrups are 1⅓ times as sweet as sugar. Conversely, this means you would use ¾ the amount of syrup as you would of sugar, but honestly, I'd go by taste.

EZ-Sweetz Liquid Sucralose

For plain sweetness, with no overtone of another flavor, I use EZ-Sweetz liquid sucralose, EZ-Sweetz Stevia & Monk Fruit blend, or NuNaturals Pure Liquid Lo Han Supreme (lo han is another name for monk fruit). I do have granular sucralose on hand in the big, yellow bag—but I haven't used it in any of these recipes. The maltodextrin used to bulk the super-sweet sucralose so that it will measure the same as sugar adds carbs. If it's just a matter of a teaspoon of the stuff, I wouldn't sweat it. But any appreciable quantity of such a sweetener will have enough maltodextrin to skew the carb/protein/fat ratios, aka the "macros."

Again, if you use zero carb liquid sucralose you need to know the sweetness equivalence. EZ-Sweetz, the brand I use, comes in two concentrations, one that is 1 drop = 1 teaspoon sugar, and one that is 1 drop = 2 teaspoons of sugar. Obviously, this makes a big difference! Read the website or package information to be sure which strength you have. I find the 1 drop = 1 teaspoon version more useful, because I often want just a touch of sweetness.

Erythritol

I use erythritol when I think it will make a contribution to the texture of a recipe. I can't recommend substituting stevia or sucralose for erythritol. Some people prefer xylitol, and I'm not against the stuff. However, I don't use it for two reasons. First, xylitol is absorbed, though slowly and incompletely, while erythritol is passed through the body unchanged, making it effectively zero-carb. And second, xylitol is profoundly toxic to dogs, and I have three. I can't risk accidental poisoning. (And no, this does not mean xylitol is poisonous to humans, anymore than the fact that chocolate is toxic to dogs means it poisonous to humans.) My friend Caitlin Weeks, aka Grass Fed Girl, with whom I wrote the CarbSmart Grain Free, Sugar Free Living Cookbook uses specifically birch xylitol to avoid GMOs. I don't share Caitlin's concern, but if you do, GMO-free erythritol is available through—you guessed it—Amazon.com.

Erythritol is roughly 60% as sweet as sugar. However, there are erythritol/stevia and erythritol/sucralose blends that measure like sugar. I'm quite fond of <u>Swerve</u>, a blend of erythritol and oligosaccharides, a sweet form of fiber, and generally measure it like sugar.

Another new sweetener blend is <u>LC-White Sugar Sweetener with Erythritol by LC Foods</u>. This product is similar to Swerve but less expensive. It also contains erythritol and oligosaccharides but also adds natural organic stevia rebaudiana leaf herbal extract and natural luo han guo monk fruit.

Don't substitute erythritol for liquid stevia or coffee flavoring syrup in a cold recipe, especially a beverage like my <u>Chocolate Milk</u> recipe on page 76. It won't dissolve well, yielding a gritty product.

Sweetener Conversions

For conversion, first you'll need to know basic measurements:

- 3 teaspoons = 1 tablespoon
- 2 tablespoons = 1 fluid ounce*
- 4 tablespoons = 2 fluid ounces = ¼ cup
- 8 fluid ounces = 1 cup

* Even if you're measuring solids! We're talking volume, not weight. A whole big yellow bag of granular sucralose sweetener has almost 92 fluid ounces in it, but weighs only 9.7 ounces. Yet a similar-sized bag of erythritol weighs 5 pounds.

Sweetness Equivalences

The following roughly equal 1 teaspoon of sugar in sweetness:

- 6 drops <u>NOW brand</u> or <u>Sweetleaf brand</u> liquid stevia
- 4 drops EZ-Sweetz brand liquid stevia or <u>stevia/monk fruit blend</u>
- ½ drop EZ-Sweetz liquid sucralose in the <u>0.2 ounce</u>, <u>0.5 ounce</u>, or <u>0.75 ounce</u> bottle
- 1 drop EZ-Sweetz liquid sucralose in the 0.66 ounce, <u>1.05 ounce</u>, or <u>2.0 ounce</u> bottle
- 1 teaspoon <u>granular sucralose</u>
- 1½ teaspoons <u>erythritol</u>
- ¾ teaspoon <u>DaVinci Gourmet sugar-free syrup</u>, all sugar-free flavors

Armed with this and some 5th grade arithmetic skills, you should be able to figure out substitutions. Or, as I said, you can just go by taste. I often do.

On Recipes That Make More Than One Serving

by Dana Carpender

In the **Fat Fast Cookbook**, many of my recipes made a single serving. Some of these do, too, but this book contains more recipes that make multiple servings. More and more, I find myself making one or two Fat Fast recipes that make 4-5 servings, and then drawing on them for a day or two. It's a nice, mindless way to do this. A few of these recipes come out fairly close to 1,000 calories for the whole batch. With those, I often just make one, and eat small servings of that and only that throughout the day, then make something else the next day.

Of course, your family may want to get in on the action, especially with things like <u>Avocado-Bacon Soup</u> on page 69 and <u>Jalapeno Poppers on the Range</u> on page 65. That's between you and them.

I am trusting you will be able to eyeball one quarter or one fifth of a given recipe. Surprisingly often, this comes out to ½ cup, but use your judgment, and be honest with yourself.

A Few New
Fat Fast Ingredients

by Dana Carpender

The nature of being a low-carber means that we give up using the ingredients we've been eating most of our life—usually highly processed and packaged foods—for better, healthier ingredients. Normally that means we eat meats, fish, veggies, and dairy everyday. Some of these foods are in this book but during a Fat Fast, we have to choose other specialized ingredients.

So throughout this cookbook, you'll see ingredients listed with an underline—like full-fat canned coconut milk. When you see these underlined ingredients, go to the CarbSmart.com website for links where to find the items:

https://www.carbsmart.com/ffc2

MEDIUM CHAIN TRIGLYCERIDE (MCT) OIL

One or two recipes in the original Fat Fast Cookbook used liquid coconut oil. I haven't used it much since. Why? I have switched to medium chain triglyceride oil, aka MCT oil. This is oil made from the most ketogenic, energy-boosting fraction of coconut oil. From a cook's perspective, the great thing about MCT oil is that, unlike coconut oil, it is liquid at room temperature, and also quite bland. That makes MCT oil a great choice for mayonnaise and other dressings where you don't want an overwhelming taste of either olive oil or coconut. When I eat a Fat Fast meal heavily laced with mayonnaise made with MCT oil (see Fat Fast Ketonnaise recipe on page 82), my Ketonix breath ketone meter registers deep ketosis by a few hours later.

A word of warning: I have seen hugely varying prices for the stuff, so pay attention. I buy Piping Rock brand through Amazon.com. At this writing it runs $26 per half gallon, on a par with extra virgin olive oil. A half-gallon lasts me several months. On the far end of the spectrum, I have seen a single liter of MCT oil priced at $90. So shop around. If you are looking for a smaller bottle, another popular brand is Now Sports MCT Oil.

NUTRITIONAL YEAST FLAKES

Just one recipe in this book calls for <u>nutritional yeast flakes</u>. I know this sounds odd, but yeast is a terrific source of umami, the same savory, mouth-filling taste we get from things like soy sauce, aged cheeses, anchovies, and mushrooms. I bought mine from the bulk bin at Bloomingfoods, my local health food coop, but any brand should do.

This is not the same as the active dry yeast used for baking—nutritional yeast is dead, not active. This means it won't grow inside you, causing nasty yeast infections. Some people with chronic yeast infection problems need to avoid even this dried version, but for most of you it should be no problem. And it's darned nutritious, too.

GUAR GUM, XANTHAN GUM, AND GLUCOMANNAN THICKENERS

These three odd sounding items, <u>guar gum</u>, <u>xanthan gum</u>, and <u>glucomannan powder</u> are thickeners made from finely milled soluble fibers. They add a velvety texture to soups, smoothies and sauces. Since these thickeners consist only of fiber, they can be discounted on a Fat Fast.

I consider these three pretty much interchangeable, and can get them all at my local health food stores. Keep an old salt shaker filled with one of these thickeners by the stove. When you want to thicken something, start whisking first, then sprinkle the thickener lightly over the surface. If you just dump in some thickener and *then* whisk, you'll get lumps.

Use a light hand with these thickeners, and stop when your dish is not quite as thick as you want—they continue to thicken on standing.

POURABLE COCONUT MILK

Overwhelmingly, I use <u>full-fat canned coconut milk</u>. I have tried the pourable stuff in a carton—you know, the stuff that's in the cooler alongside the almond and soy milks. I bought the unsweetened version, naturally. The macros—percentage of fat to everything else—were fine. However, it was watery and flavorless; I cannot imagine what the appeal is. However, if you like it, feel free—again, so long as you buy the unsweetened version, and keep track of your portions.

The one use I did find for pourable coconut milk was thinning out canned coconut milk for beverages. But I didn't see enough of a difference between the pourable coconut milk and plain ol' water to bother purchasing it again.

NUTS

The best place to find pecans, macadamia nuts and any other nut is Nuts.com, a family business now in its third generation. Besides the half dozen various nuts and seeds listed in this cookbook, they have hundreds of other items from chocolates and sweets to coffees, teas, and baking ingredients.

PECANS

1 ounce pecans (¼ cup) will have: 189 Calories; 19g Fat (85.4% calories from fat); 2g Protein; 5g Carbohydrate; 2g Dietary Fiber; 3g Usable Carbs

MACADAMIA NUTS

1 ounce macadamia nuts (¼ cup) will have: 199 Calories; 21g Fat (88.3% calories from fat); 2g Protein; 4g Carbohydrate; 3g Dietary Fiber; 1g Usable Carbs

OLIVES

20 large olives marinated in 2 teaspoons olive oil will have: 181 Calories; 18g Fat (87.2% calories from fat); 1g Protein; 5g Carbohydrate; 3g Dietary Fiber; 2g Usable Carbs (You could just buy olives packed in olive oil, you know.)

PATE DE FOIE GRAS

If you're feeling wealthy and have a really good gourmet food shop in the neighborhood, 1 ½ ounces pate de foie gras will have: 196 Calories; 19g Fat (86.0% calories from fat); 5g Protein; 2g Carbohydrate; 0g Dietary Fiber; 2g Usable Carbs

FAT SNACKS

You'll think I've gone right 'round the bend, but I buy beef fat, cut it in strips, put it on my broiler rack, and bake it till it's crisp and brown. Then I salt it and eat it. I don't know the exact fat percentage here, because it will depend on how much fat cooks out of your, well, fat—there will actually be some protein in there, too. Still, this has served me well. Figure 1 ounce after cooking is a serving, and count it at 250 calories.

CREAM CHEESE

2 ounces cream cheese will have: 198 Calories; 20g Fat (88.5% calories from fat); 4g Protein; 2g Carbohydrate; 0g Dietary Fiber; 2g Usable Carbs

SUGAR FREE GELATIN WITH HEAVY CREAM

1 serving prepared sugar-free, gelatin dessert with ¼ cup of heavy cream, whipped, will have: 214 Calories; 22g Fat (90.7% calories from fat); 3g Protein; 2g Carbohydrate; 0g Dietary Fiber; 2g Usable Carbs

BONE BROTH RECIPE

Several recipes in this book call for broth. You can use packaged broth if you like, though I urge you to read the labels. "Broths" are often more like chemical soup. Two brands I like are Kitchen Basics and Kirkland Organic (the Costco house brand).

However, homemade bone broth is so cheap and easy to make, and such a valuable addition to your diet, that making it is more than worth your while. This is not so much a recipe as simply a description of how I make bone broth:

- First of all, it helps to buy meat on the bone! Rotisserie chicken, wings, cut up chicken with the bones in and the skin on, will all yield bones. Don't worry if they're picked completely clean. Naked bones will make remarkably rich and flavorful broth.

- Stash your bones in a plastic bag in the freezer—I use a plastic grocery sack. Throw in any onion or celery trimmings you might have.

- When you have enough bones to fill your slow cooker to the brim, dump them in. Cover them with water, add just a little salt—I use a rounded teaspoon of good mined sea salt in my big 5 quart slow cooker. Also add a tablespoon or two of cider or wine vinegar. This will help draw calcium out of the bones, making a calcium-rich broth.

- Slap the top on your slow cooker, shove it to an out-of-the-way corner of your kitchen, set it to low, and let it cook for a good two days. No, I am not kidding. Then turn off the slow cooker and let the whole thing cool with the lid still on. Put your colander into your biggest bowl and use this to strain your broth.

- That's it. Toss the bones and stash your broth in snap-top containers in the freezer to draw upon as needed. Half-cup containers are ideal; you can just grab as many as your recipe calls for.

Recipes Under 80% Fat

We have here a few recipes that come in at just under the 80% fat mark, but were too good to leave out. Be sure to balance them with something from the 90% fat or above range.

Buttered Pork Rinds

By Dana Carpender

Based on the famous Chex Mix, these are delicious. The hardest part will be keeping yourself to eating only a few at a time. Remember, this is 12 servings.

Servings: 12

Ingredients

½ cup butter (1 stick)

2 tablespoons Worcestershire sauce

½ teaspoon onion powder

½ teaspoon garlic powder

½ teaspoon paprika

1 teaspoon salt

3½ ounces <u>pork skins</u>,
you can get bags just this size

Instructions

- Preheat oven to 250° F. Put the butter in a big roasting pan, and stick it into the heating oven to melt.

- When the butter is melted, stir in the Worcestershire sauce and all the seasonings, combining it all well.

- Now dump in the pork rinds, and toss them in the seasoned butter, coating them as evenly as you can.

- Stick 'em in the oven, and set the timer for 20 minutes.

- When the timer beeps, toss your rinds again. Put them back in the oven, and set the timer for another 20 minutes.

- Now pull out one rind and let it cool a bit. Test it to see if it's good and crunchy. If it is, they're done. If not, repeat the tossing and roasting for up to another 30 minutes.

- Store in an airtight container. Put it in a high place to avoid blowing past your limits.

Nutritionals

Per Serving: 116 Calories; 10g Fat (79.6% calories from fat); 5g Protein; 1g Carbohydrate; trace Dietary Fiber; 29mg Cholesterol; 432mg Sodium.

Avocado Soup

By Dana Carpender

Super-quick and easy, and great for a sweaty summer day. If you're not going to eat it all in one day you might share it. You know how avocados darken.

Servings: 3

Ingredients

1 avocado, small, black, ripe
(The big, smooth-skinned green ones have more carbs and less fat.)

¾ cup sour cream, divided

2 cups chicken broth, chilled

Salt and pepper, to taste

2 tablespoons minced cilantro, optional

Hot sauce, to taste, optional

Instructions

- Split the avocado, remove the pit, and use a spoon to scoop the flesh into your food processor or blender.

- Add ½ cup of the sour cream and all of the chicken broth. Run until you have a smooth, creamy soup.

- Salt and pepper to taste.

- Top each serving with a rounded tablespoon of sour cream and a couple of teaspoons of cilantro. Pass the hot sauce!

Nutritionals

Per Serving: 257 Calories; 23g Fat (78.4% calories from fat); 6g Protein; 8g Carbohydrate; 2g Dietary Fiber; 26mg Cholesterol; 546mg Sodium.

Curried Chicken Noodle Bowl

By Dana Carpender

It's easy to make the soup/sauce part of this and heat up the noodles, stashing the leftovers in the fridge for another quick feeding. This is good without the shirataki, too, but the portion is obviously smaller.

Servings: 3

Ingredients

1 teaspoon curry powder, or to taste

1 tablespoon butter

1 cup chicken broth

1 cup full-fat canned coconut milk, unsweetened

1 teaspoon chicken bouillon concentrate

⅛ teaspoon garlic powder, scant

2 packages shirataki noodles, I use the fettuccini, but any of 'em would do.

Glucomannan powder, guar gum or xanthan gum, sprinkled in to desired thickness as described in our Thickeners section on page 42

1½ tablespoons slivered almonds, toasted (optional)

Instructions

- In a saucepan, sauté the curry powder in the butter for just a couple of minutes.

- Add the chicken broth, coconut milk, bouillon concentrate, and garlic powder, and whisk to combine. Bring to a low simmer.

- Prepare your shirataki as described in the Preparing Shirataki Noodles section on pages 35 & 36.

- Thicken the soup to taste with guar gum or xanthan gum. I like it about the texture of heavy cream.

- Drain the noodles again, then return them to the bowl. Pour the soup over them and top with the almonds. Done!

Nutritionals
Per Serving: 252 Calories; 23g Fat (79.7% calories from fat); 6g Protein; 8g Carbohydrate; 3g Dietary Fiber; 10mg Cholesterol; 453mg Sodium.

Blue Cheese Carbonara

By Dana Carpender

This is the sort of thing you might get at a good Italian restaurant—minus the carbs, of course. Sheer luxury on a plate.

Servings: 1

Ingredients

1 package tofu shirataki, <u>fettuccini</u> style

1 bacon slice

1½ tablespoons whipped cream cheese

2 tablespoons crumbled blue cheese—gorgonzola is good, here

1 egg yolk

1 pinch garlic powder

Salt and pepper, to taste

Instructions

- Prepare your shirataki as described in the <u>Preparing Shirataki Noodles</u> section on pages 35 & 36.

- In the meanwhile, snip up your bacon and start it frying over medium heat in a medium-sized skillet. Measure the cream cheese and blue cheese, and separate your egg. (You won't be making meringues while Fat Fasting, so may as well feed the white to the dog.)

- When the bacon is crisp, remove it from the skillet with a slotted spoon, and reserve on a small plate.

- Pour the bacon grease over the noodles, and add the egg yolk. Use two forks to toss like mad, as the residual heat from the noodles cooks this into a creamy sauce.

- Add the cream cheese, blue cheese, and garlic powder, and toss until the cream cheese is melted in, and just a few hunks of blue cheese remain.

- Crumble in bacon.

- Salt and pepper to taste, and dive in.

Nutritionals

Per Serving: 209 Calories; 18g Fat (79.6% calories from fat); 9g Protein; 1g Carbohydrate; trace Dietary Fiber; 249mg Cholesterol; 408mg Sodium.

Caesar Salad with Olives and Pine Nuts

By Dana Carpender

I stole this idea from Truffles, a terrific restaurant here in Bloomington. Do use good quality olives—I used half green, half black, packed in olive oil, from our superb local gourmet grocery Sahara Mart.

Servings: 1

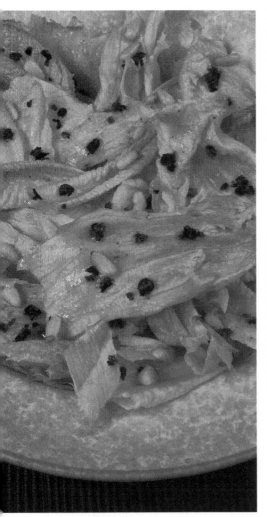

Ingredients

2 cups torn lettuce leaves, romaine hearts

1½ tablespoons <u>Caesar Dressing</u> recipe on page 84

3 olives, pitted and chopped

2 tablespoons <u>pine nuts</u>, toasted

Instructions

- Easy! Put your lettuce in a mixing bowl or salad bowl.

- Add the dressing, and toss like mad till every leaf is coated. Plate it, top with the olives and pine nuts, and you're done.

Nutritionals
Per Serving: 230 Calories; 21g Fat (79.4% calories from fat); 5g Protein; 7g Carbohydrate; 3g Dietary Fiber; trace Cholesterol; 368mg Sodium.

Notes
To toast your pine nuts, just stir them in a small, dry skillet over medium low heat until they're touched with gold.

Dana's Fat Fast Chili

By Dana Carpender

Chili sans tomatoes is traditional in Texas, so that's where I started. It was surprising the lengths I had to go to, getting the fat level of this recipe high enough for our purposes, and it's still only 79%. Still, it's darned tasty.

Servings: 8

Ingredients

1 pound ground beef, 70/30

6 tablespoons bacon grease

8 ounces mushrooms, chopped

8 teaspoons chili powder

2 teaspoons paprika

1 tablespoon onion powder

1 teaspoon garlic powder

2 teaspoons cumin

4 drops English Toffee liquid stevia

1 tablespoon cider vinegar

1 cup beef broth

12 tablespoons sour cream

Instructions

- In your big, heavy skillet, over medium heat, start browning and breaking up the ground beef in the bacon grease. When it's about half-browned, throw in the mushrooms. (I actually buy sliced mushrooms, and break them up with the edge of my spatula as I go. Easier than chopping.)

- When the beef is browned, add everything else but the sour cream and stir it all up. DO NOT DRAIN THE FAT!! Turn the burner to low and let it all simmer for 25-30 minutes.

- Serve with 1½ tablespoons of sour cream on each portion.

Nutritionals
Per Serving: 349 Calories; 30g Fat (79% calories from fat); 13g Protein; 6g Carbohydrate; 1g Dietary Fiber; 68mg Cholesterol; 292mg Sodium.

Notes
The mushrooms here serve to soak up some of the fat. Still, this is definitely greasy chili, and we loved it. The portions are quite small, about ½ cup. I like to turn mine into chili-mac by serving it over tofu shirataki macaroni, but That Nice Boy I Married was fine with it straight up, with the sour cream.

Even this small serving has 349 calories, and it's only 79% fat, so adjust your intake for the rest of the day accordingly.

Cream of Chicken Soup Italiano

By Dana Carpender

Creamy and yummy! Perfect for a cold, rainy night. This is a fine illustration of how even seemingly non-carby ingredients such as broth and seasonings do, in fact, have a little carbohydrate. MasterCook, the software program we use to compute our nutritionals, counts a gram for the broth alone. Read labels and you may be able to drop it just a little.

Servings: 1

Ingredients

1 cup chicken broth, good and strong

½ clove garlic, crushed

½ teaspoon dried oregano

¼ teaspoon red pepper flakes, optional

2 ounces cream cheese

1 teaspoon tomato paste

Instructions

- Easy! In a saucepan, over medium heat, bring the chicken broth, garlic, oregano, and red pepper flakes, if using, to a low simmer. Let 'em cook for about 5 minutes.

- Add the cream cheese and tomato paste, and whisk until they're completely dissolved/melted. Pour into a cup and it's done.

Nutritionals

Per Serving: 243 Calories; 21g Fat (78.1% calories from fat); 9g Protein; 4g Carbohydrate; 1g Dietary Fiber; 62mg Cholesterol; 974mg Sodium.

Mushroom Eggs

By Dana Carpender

Another recipe where the mushroom not only seasons, but helps hold fat.

Servings: 1

Ingredients

1 mushroom, sliced

1 tablespoon bacon grease

1 pinch onion powder

1 pinch garlic powder

2 eggs

Instructions

- Slice or chop your mushroom. In a medium non-stick skillet (or one you've coated with cooking spray), sauté the mushroom in the bacon grease. When it's starting to soften, stir in the onion powder and garlic powder.

- Scramble up your eggs, dump them into the skillet, and stir till set. That's it!

Nutritionals

Per Serving: 255 Calories; 22g Fat (78.5% calories from fat); 11g Protein; 2g Carbohydrate; trace Dietary Fiber; 387mg Cholesterol; 183mg Sodium.

Sesame-Almond Chicken Noodle Salad

By Dana Carpender

Always a favorite flavor combination of mine, this reminds me of a (very carby) salad I bought years ago at my neighborhood health food store in Chicago.

Servings: 4

Ingredients

1 package tofu shirataki, I used <u>fettuccini</u> style

¼ cup <u>slivered almonds</u>, or sliced

½ tablespoon <u>coconut oil</u>

½ cup diced chicken

¼ cup diced celery

2 scallions, sliced thin, including the crisp part of the green shoot

2 tablespoons <u>almond butter</u>

2 tablespoons mayonnaise or <u>Fat Fast Ketonnaise</u> recipe on page 82

2 teaspoons soy sauce

1 teaspoon dark sesame oil

Instructions

- Prepare your shirataki as described in the <u>Preparing Shirataki Noodles</u> section on pages 35 & 36.

- While the noodles are nuking, sauté the almonds in the coconut oil until nicely golden, then remove from the heat.

- In a mixing bowl, assemble the chicken, celery, and scallions. When the noodles and almonds are cool enough not to cook the celery and scallions, dump 'em in.

- In a smaller bowl, whisk together the almond butter, mayo, soy sauce, and dark sesame oil. Pour this over the salad, using a rubber scraper to get all of it—after all, this is where your fat content is coming from.

- Stir until everything is well-coated, and it's done.

Nutritionals
Per Serving: 241 Calories; 22g Fat (78.6% calories from fat); 9g Protein; 4g Carbohydrate; 2g Dietary Fiber; 24mg Cholesterol; 258mg Sodium.

Artichoke and Mushroom "Risotto"

By Dana Carpender

Boy, have I been having fun with Miracle Rice! This is not only a great Fat Fast dish as-is, but would make a fine side dish with chicken, or you could add diced leftover chicken to turn it into a main dish. But not for Fat Fasting; it would mess up your ratios.

Servings: 3

Ingredients

1 package Miracle Rice

6 ounces canned artichoke hearts, chopped

2 mushrooms, chopped

1 scallion, sliced

¼ cup pine nuts

3 tablespoons butter, divided

1 teaspoon chicken bouillon concentrate

2 tablespoons heavy cream

Instructions

- Prepare your Miracle Rice as described in the Preparing Shirataki Noodles section on pages 35 & 36. While it's microwaving, chop up the veggies.

- Put your big, heavy skillet over medium-low heat. Add the pine nuts, and stir them in the dry skillet until they're a pretty gold. Remove them to a saucer and keep them nearby.

- With your skillet back over the burner, melt the butter and throw in the mushrooms and scallions. Sauté until the mushrooms have softened and changed color. Stir in the artichoke hearts.

- Surely your Miracle Rice is ready by now! Dump it into the skillet, add the bouillon concentrate and cream, and stir the whole thing up, making sure the bouillon concentrate dissolves and everything is evenly coated.

- Stir in the pine nuts, and that's it!

Nutritionals

Per Serving: 228 Calories; 21g Fat (79.8% calories from fat); 5g Protein; 7g Carbohydrate; 1g Dietary Fiber; 45mg Cholesterol; 388mg Sodium.

Recipes 80% to 83% Fat

In the general run of things, these are certainly high fat recipes. But for Fat-Fasting, they're at the bottom of the range. So enjoy these recipes, but be sure to balance them from something higher fat at another "feeding."

Mac and Pepper Cheese

By Dana Carpender

A great recipe deserves a variation. Having loved the macaroni and cheese recipe in the first Fat Fast book, and being an inveterate chili-head, I came up with this. If you'd like it even hotter, use jalapeno jack cheese.

Servings: 1

Ingredients

1 package tofu shirataki, <u>macaroni</u> shaped

¼ cup shredded Monterey jack cheese

1 tablespoon heavy cream

1 tablespoon whipped cream cheese

2 teaspoons minced jalapeno pepper, canned or jarred, not fresh

Instructions

- Prepare your shirataki as described in the <u>Preparing Shirataki Noodles</u> section on pages 35 & 36.

- When you've drained the noodles that last time, stir in the other ingredients until they melt together into a sauce (with little bits of jalapeno in it, of course). If you need to zap it an extra 30 seconds, go ahead, then stir a little more.

Nutritionals

Per Serving: 193 Calories; 18g Fat (81.4% calories from fat); 8g Protein; 1g Carbohydrate; trace Dietary Fiber; 58mg Cholesterol; 200mg Sodium.

80% to 83%

Liverwurst Stuffed Celery

By Dana Carpender

I adore liverwurst, and it's hugely nutritious, what with being made from liver and all. Add a dash of <u>Tabasco</u> to this if you like, but it's hardly necessary. This is a super-easy faux pate. A word to the wise: My grocery store carries two brands of liverwurst, one with 1 gram of carbohydrate per serving, and one with 3 grams of carbohydrate per serving. Read the labels!

Servings: 1

Ingredients

1 ounce braunschweiger

1 ounce cream cheese, room temperature

1 large celery rib

Instructions

- Use a fork to mash and mix the braunschweiger and cream cheese together until completely blended.

- Stuff into your celery, and snarf it down.

Nutritionals
Per Serving: 207 Calories; 19g Fat (82.1% calories from fat); 6g Protein; 3g Carbohydrate; 1g Dietary Fiber; 75mg Cholesterol; 443mg Sodium.

80% to 83%

Bacon-Pecan Spaghetti

By Dana Carpender

I was trying to come up with something to do with shirataki that didn't have even a hint of Italian. This was wonderful, easily good enough to make for the family as a side dish even if you're not Fat Fasting.

Servings: 1

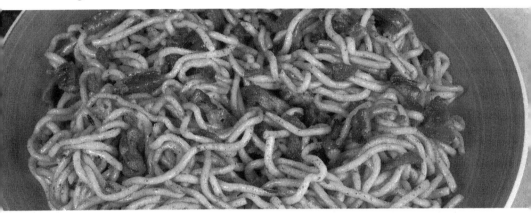

Ingredients

1 package tofu shirataki, spaghetti

2 slices bacon

1 teaspoon bacon grease

2 tablespoons chopped pecans

¾ teaspoon Tony Chachere's Original Creole Seasoning

1 teaspoon minced parsley

Instructions

- Prepare your shirataki as described in the Preparing Shirataki Noodles section on pages 35 & 36.

- In the meanwhile, use your kitchen shears to snip the bacon into a medium-sized skillet over medium heat. Fry your bacon bits crisp.

- While the bacon's cooking, quickly chop your pecans.

- When the bacon is done, scoop it out with a slotted spoon, and put it on a little plate to hold. Add the extra bacon grease to the grease in the skillet, throw in the pecans, and stir them in the fat for about 5 minutes, until they smell toasty. Stir in the Creole seasoning.

- By now your noodles are ready! Drain them that one last time, then add the bacon and pecans, using a rubber scraper to scrape every drop of bacon grease over the noodles.

- Quickly mince your parsley, I'd just use the kitchen shears to snip it into the bowl, stir it in, and you're done.

Nutritionals
Per Serving: 219 Calories; 21g Fat (82.7% calories from fat); 5g Protein; 4g Carbohydrate; 2g Dietary Fiber; 15mg Cholesterol; 388mg Sodium.

80% to 83%

Broccoli with Lemon Yeast Butter

By Dana Carpender

You're going to think I'm crazy, with the nutritional yeast. It has an unpleasant reputation left over from the 1970s, when people were foolishly adding it to juice or protein shakes. This is a bad idea. Nutritional yeast is incompatible with sweet stuff. But it's a terrific source of umami, the rich, mouth-filling savoriness we treasure in aged cheeses, soy sauce, mushrooms, anchovies, and many other favorite foods, which makes it a great seasoning here.

Servings: 1

Ingredients

1 cup broccoli

2 tablespoons butter

1 teaspoon lemon juice

1 teaspoon <u>nutritional yeast flakes</u>

Salt, to taste

Instructions

- Super-easy! Steam your broccoli until just barely tender, and still brilliantly green. Overcooked broccoli is an abomination before the Lord.

- In the meanwhile, melt the butter and stir in the lemon juice and nutritional yeast flakes.

- When the broccoli is done, plonk it in a dish, pour the sauce over it, salt to taste, and devour. Wonder why you've been avoiding nutritional yeast all these years.

Nutritionals
Per Serving: 238 Calories; 24g Fat (83.4% calories from fat); 5g Protein; 6g Carbohydrate; 3g Dietary Fiber; 62mg Cholesterol; 255mg Sodium.

Buffalo Chicken Soup

By Dana Carpender

This soup is devastating. I've analyzed this as 10 servings, but unless you live alone, you won't get that much. The family will eat it all, while you're sticking to your Fat Fast portions—which should be about 1½ cups each.

Servings: 10   Yield: 16 cups

Ingredients

¼ medium onion, minced

1 clove garlic, crushed

1 quart chicken broth

1 cup heavy cream

4 ounces cream cheese, cut in 1" cubes

1 cup shredded Colby Jack cheese

5 ounces crumbled blue cheese, divided

½ cup diced chicken, cooked

2 tablespoons Frank's hot sauce

Instructions

- Mince your onion and crush your garlic into a large, heavy-bottomed saucepan. Add the chicken broth, put it over a medium burner, and bring it to a boil. Now turn it down to a low simmer, and let it go till the onion is soft, about 20-30 minutes.

- Add the heavy cream and whisk it in. Whisk in the cream cheese, a few cubes at a time.

- Now whisk in the Colby Jack cheese, a handful at a time, making sure each addition is melted in before adding more. Now do the same with about half of the blue cheese.

- Stir in your chicken and the hot sauce.

- Just before serving, stir in the extra blue cheese in. Feel free to add another dash or two of hot sauce at the table!

Nutritionals

Per Serving: 213 Calories; 19g Fat (80.3% calories from fat); 8g Protein; 2g Carbohydrate; trace Dietary Fiber; 64mg Cholesterol; 628mg Sodium.

Fettuccini Carbonara

By Dana Carpender

Yummy, creamy, smoky, this is a classic.

Servings: 1

Ingredients

2 slices bacon

1 packet tofu shirataki, <u>fettuccini</u> shape

1½ tablespoons heavy cream

1 egg yolk

1 tablespoon grated Parmesan cheese

⅛ teaspoon pepper

Instructions

- Use your kitchen shears to snip the bacon into a skillet over medium heat.

- In the meanwhile, prepare your shirataki as described in the <u>Preparing Shirataki Noodles</u> section on pages 35 & 36.

- Stir your bacon!

- Okay, bacon's crisp and the noodles are fully drained. Pour the bacon grease and cream into the noodles, then add the yolk. Immediately toss madly with two forks until the sauce is smooth and creamy.

- Stir in the bacon bits, Parmesan cheese, and pepper, and devour.

Nutritionals

Per Serving: 233 Calories; 21g Fat (81.8% calories from fat); 9g Protein; 1g Carbohydrate; trace Dietary Fiber; 258mg Cholesterol; 311mg Sodium.

Parmesan Stuffed Mushrooms

By Dana Carpender

Both mushrooms and Parmesan cheese are rich sources of umami, making these mushrooms deliciously savory and satisfying. Triple or quadruple the recipe and you can take 'em to parties!

Servings: 6

Ingredients

3 tablespoons olive oil

3 cloves garlic

12 ounces mushrooms

8 ounces cream cheese, room temperature

¼ cup grated Parmesan cheese, divided

¼ teaspoon pepper

¼ teaspoon onion powder

¼ teaspoon cayenne

Instructions

- Preheat oven to 350° F. Put 1 tablespoon of the olive oil in an 8" x 8" pan and slosh it about to coat the bottom.

- Put the garlic in the food processor, and pulse until it is chopped fairly fine.

- Wipe the mushrooms clean with a damp paper towel. Remove the stems and drop them into your food processor with the garlic. Set the caps aside for the moment.

- Pulse the food processor again, finely chopping the stems and mixing them in with the garlic.

- Put your large, heavy skillet over medium heat. When it's hot, add the remaining 2 tablespoons of olive oil, and dump in the mushroom-garlic mixture. Sauté until the mushrooms have exuded their liquid and it has evaporated.

- Cut the cream cheese in chunks, and melt them into the mushroom stem mixture one at a time. Mix in 2 tablespoons of the Parmesan, plus the seasonings.

- When the mushroom-cheese mixture is evenly blended, stuff it into the caps, filling each generously. Arrange in the prepared pan as they're filled.

- Sprinkle the remaining Parmesan lightly over the stuffed mushrooms. Bake for 45 minutes, or until lightly golden.

- Eat 'em hot! They reheat nicely in the microwave. Figure about 3-4 mushrooms to a serving, depending on the size of your mushrooms, of course.

Nutritionals

Per Serving: 224 Calories; 21g Fat (82.9% calories from fat); 5g Protein; 4g Carbohydrate; 1g Dietary Fiber; 44mg Cholesterol; 176mg Sodium.

Saganaki

By Dana Carpender

Greek restaurant saganaki is not pretty but tastes amazing! Saganaki often includes a dramatic flaming with brandy, accompanied by a cry of "Opa!", but this simpler version is great. Lick all the lemony butter-and-cheese-fat off the plate, to keep your fat percentage up.

Servings: 1

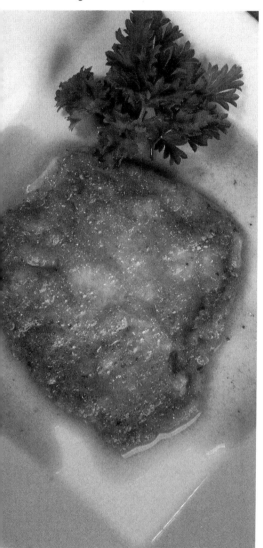

Ingredients

1 ounce kasseri cheese

1 tablespoon butter

1 lemon wedge

Instructions

- Cut your kasseri in a slice about ¼" thick.

- Put a smallish heavy-bottomed skillet over medium heat. If it's not non-stick, give it a squirt of non-stick cooking spray, first. When the skillet is hot, add the butter and slosh it about as it melts. Add the cheese, and fry it till it's golden brown on one side, about 4-5 minutes, then flip and fry the other side.

- Plate the cheese, scraping all the butter from the skillet over it. Squeeze the lemon wedge over it before nomming it down.

Nutritionals

Per Serving: 212 Calories; 21g Fat (83.7% calories from fat); 7g Protein; 2g Carbohydrate; trace Dietary Fiber; 59mg Cholesterol; 385mg Sodium.

Jalapeno Poppers on the Range

By Dana Carpender

Take your average Jalapeno Poppers, add ranch-style seasonings to the cheese, and you get Jalapeno Poppers on the Range! You've seen this sort of thing before, but you might not have realized these were perfect Fat Fast fare. Double, triple, quadruple the recipe, and warm them up later. Or share, if you're feeling particularly generous.

Servings: 4

Ingredients

8 jalapeno chile peppers

8 bacon slices

8 ounces cream cheese, room temperature

1 teaspoon minced parsley

2 teaspoons minced onion

¼ teaspoon salt

¼ teaspoon pepper

¼ teaspoon dried dill weed

¼ teaspoon dried thyme

Instructions

- 30 minutes before assembling your poppers, put a handful of toothpicks to soak in water.

- Put the cream cheese in your food processor along with all the seasonings. Run until evenly blended. At this point, it's easiest if you chill the cream cheese mixture before stuffing it into peppers.

- Coat your broiler rack with non-stick cooking spray. Slit your jalapenos and flick out the seeds and white pith. Stuff with the seasoned cream cheese.

- Wrap each jalapeno tightly in a bacon slice, fastening with toothpicks. Arrange them on the broiler rack as you go.

- Now wash your hands very thoroughly with soap and water before you do anything else, or you will regret it the next

time you touch your eyes or nose.

- Broil close to the heat, turning from time to time with a tongs, until the bacon is crisp.

- Eat your two poppers, and hide the rest from the family! Then you can reheat 'em for your next three feedings.

Nutritionals

Per Serving: 281 Calories; 26g Fat (83.0% calories from fat); 9g Protein; 4g Carbohydrate; 1g Dietary Fiber; 73mg Cholesterol; 504mg Sodium.

Mac 'n' Nacho Cheese

By Dana Carpender

The mac 'n' cheese in the original Fat Fast book was so popular, I figured I'd give you a variation. Yum!

Servings: 1

Ingredients

1 package tofu shirataki, I'd use macaroni style

½ ounce shredded cheddar cheese

3 tablespoons whipped cream cheese

1 pinch paprika

1 pinch garlic powder

1 pinch onion powder

1 pinch cayenne

Instructions

- Prepare your shirataki as described in the Preparing Shirataki Noodles section on pages 35 & 36.

- When they're fully drained, put them back in the bowl, add everything else and stir well.

- Zap 'em again for maybe 30 seconds, stir one more time, and stuff them in your face.

Nutritionals
Per Serving: 164 Calories; 15g Fat (83.1% calories from fat); 5g Protein; 2g Carbohydrate; trace Dietary Fiber; 52mg Cholesterol; 216mg Sodium.

Fat Fast Fried "Rice"

By Dana Carpender

OMG! This is so good! When you're not Fat Fasting, consider stirring bits of leftover steak, should you have any, into this, or serve it as a side dish.

Servings: 3

Ingredients

2 packages Miracle Rice

1½ ounces snow pea pods, fresh

1 tablespoon shredded carrot

2 scallions

¼ cup butter, divided

1 egg

2 tablespoons soy sauce

1 teaspoon beef bouillon concentrate

1 teaspoon dark sesame oil

Salt and pepper, to taste

Instructions

- Drain, rinse, and microwave the Miracle Rice as described in the Preparing Shirataki Noodles section on pages 35 & 36.

- Pinch the ends off the snow peas, pulling off the strings. Use your kitchen shears to cut them into ¼" lengths. Grate your tablespoon of carrot, and slice your scallions, including the crisp green part of the shoot.

- In a large skillet—preferably non-stick, but you can give your regular skillet a shot of cooking spray—melt ½ tablespoon of the butter over medium heat. Scramble up the egg, pour it into the skillet, and let it set in a sheet, flipping it once to cook both sides. Don't panic if it tears; you're going to cut it up anyway.

- Remove your sheet of egg to a plate, and put the skillet back on the burner. Melt the rest of the butter, and add the vegetables.

Sauté them for 3-4 minutes, until they're starting to soften.

- Add your Miracle Rice, the soy sauce, bouillon paste, and dark sesame oil, stirring until all the Miracle Rice is evenly coated with the seasonings.

- Chop or snip your egg into pea-sized bits, and stir that in, too. Let the whole thing cook another 5 minutes or so, stirring occasionally.

- Salt and pepper to taste, and it's done.

Nutritionals
Per Serving: 189 Calories; 18g Fat (83.7% calories from fat); 3g Protein; 5g Carbohydrate; 1g Dietary Fiber; 104mg Cholesterol; 977mg Sodium.

80% to 83%

Chicken Wing with Honey Mustard

By Dana Carpender

It seems silly to roast a single chicken wing, and the Honey Mustard Dressing/Dip recipe makes four servings. So roast four wings, make a batch of Honey Mustard Dressing/Dip, and you've got 4 feedings ready to go. And remember, when I say "four wings," I mean four whole wings. If you've got the cut-up cocktail wings like you get at restaurants you can have two pieces.

Servings: 4

Ingredients

4 chicken wings

1½ tablespoons Honey Mustard Dressing/Dip on page 96

Instructions

- Just salt and pepper the wings, or maybe sprinkle with a little Creole seasoning, and roast them at 350° F, basting now and then with the fat in the pan, until they're golden and crunchy. That's it.

- Serve with the Honey Mustard Dressing/Dip to bring 'em up to the proper fat content.

Nutritionals

Per Serving: 220 Calories; 21g Fat (82.4% calories from fat); 10g Protein; trace Carbohydrate; trace Dietary Fiber; 43mg Cholesterol; 192mg Sodium.

Avocado-Bacon Soup

By Dana Carpender

This is downright amazing, if I do say so myself. The quality of the chicken broth matters here. Both your palate and your body will thank you for keeping good, homemade bone broth on hand.

Servings: 4

Ingredients

4 slices bacon

2 tablespoons minced onion

1 clove garlic

1 cup chicken broth

1 teaspoon <u>chipotle hot sauce</u>

1 tablespoon lime juice

1 avocado

½ cup heavy cream

Salt and pepper

4 teaspoons sour cream

Cilantro

Instructions

- Put a large, heavy saucepan over medium-low heat, and use your kitchen shears to snip the bacon into it. Fry the bacon bits, stirring frequently, until they're crisp, then use a slotted spoon to remove to a plate and reserve.

- Keeping the temperature low, add the onion and garlic, and sauté in the bacon grease for 2-3 minutes.

- Add the chicken broth, hot sauce, and lime juice. Bring to a simmer and let it cook for 5 minutes or so.

- Halve your avocado, remove the pit, and use a spoon to scoop the flesh into the soup. Add back about a tablespoon of the bacon bits. Let simmer for another 4-5 minutes.

- Add the heavy cream. Then, using a stick blender, puree the soup, leaving a few teeny chunks of avocado for texture. Salt and pepper to taste; I used about ¼ teaspoon of each.

- Serve with a teaspoon of sour cream, a sprinkling of the bacon bits, and a little minced cilantro if you like it.

Nutritionals

Per Serving: 244 Calories; 23g Fat (82.5% calories from fat); 5g Protein; 6g Carbohydrate; 1g Dietary Fiber; 48mg Cholesterol; 342mg Sodium.

Notes

If you don't have homemade bone broth, read the labels on the packaged stuff. Kitchen Basics and Kirkland (Costco's house brand) are two I have used successfully. I often reduce these—let them simmer down by about —to strengthen the flavor.

Recipes 84% to 87% Fat

Not quite at that 90% ideal fat percentage, these recipes are still high enough to keep you in ketosis. Tasty too!

Chipotle Pasta Salad

By Dana Carpender

This Southwestern take on pasta salad is cooling on a hot summer day, not to mention beautiful on the plate. And delicious, of course.

Servings: 3

Ingredients

2 packages tofu shirataki, <u>macaroni</u> shape

⅓ medium cucumber, diced

⅓ cup diced red bell pepper

2 tablespoons minced red onion

½ avocado, diced

¼ cup mayonnaise or <u>Fat Fast Ketonnaise</u> recipe on page 82

2 tablespoons sour cream

1 teaspoon cider vinegar

⅛ teaspoon onion powder

⅛ teaspoon garlic powder

⅛ teaspoon paprika

2 teaspoons <u>chipotle hot sauce</u>

Salt and pepper, to taste

2 tablespoons minced cilantro

Instructions

- Prepare your shirataki as described in the <u>Preparing Shirataki Noodles</u> section on pages 35 & 36.

- In the meanwhile, dice up your vegetables —I left the skin on my cucumber for the color, but do as you like.

- Stir together everything from the mayonnaise through the hot sauce. This is your dressing.

- When your shirataki have drained for the last time, let them cool a bit. You don't want the hot noodles wilting your vegetables.

- When they're lukewarm, add the vegetables and the dressing, and stir the whole thing up. Salt and pepper to taste.

- Stir in the cilantro. Refrigerate for several hours to let the flavors marry.

Nutritionals

Per Serving: 219 Calories; 23g Fat (87.2% calories from fat); 2g Protein; 6g Carbohydrate; 2g Dietary Fiber; 11mg Cholesterol; 197mg Sodium.

Keto Mocha Shake

By Dana Carpender

This takes some planning ahead, because you need to make coffee ice cubes. But who needs Starbucks when you can make this and run?

Servings: 1

Ingredients

1 cup brewed coffee, divided

½ cup full-fat canned coconut milk, unsweetened

¼ teaspoon chocolate liquid stevia

2 teaspoons cocoa powder

⅛ teaspoon glucomannan powder, guar gum, or xanthan gum sprinkled in to desired thickness as described in our Thickeners section on page 42

Instructions

- You'll want ¾ cup of brewed coffee—good and strong—well-chilled. You want the other ¼ cup in the form of coffee ice cubes; that's 2-3 cubes in your standard ice cube tray. But then, coffee's pretty much carb- and calorie-free, so who's counting?

- Put the chilled coffee in your blender with the coconut milk, liquid stevia, and cocoa powder. Turn the blender on.

- Drop in your coffee cubes, one at a time, letting each get pulverized before adding another.

- Add ¼ teaspoon of whichever thickener you're using, then let it blend in for 30 seconds before you decide whether you need another ¼ teaspoon. When it's a little less thick than you want it—it will keep thickening on standing, not that it'll stand long—call it good. Pour it into a car cup and head out!

Nutritionals
Per Serving: 235 Calories; 24g Fat (85.8% calories from fat); 3g Protein; 6g Carbohydrate; 1g Dietary Fiber; 0mg Cholesterol; 28mg Sodium.

Iceberg Wedge with Gorgonzola Dressing and Hazelnuts

By Dana Carpender

Tres mid-20th-Century, with a little modern kick from the hazelnuts. If you're not a hazelnut fan, consider toasted pecans instead. Iceberg lettuce holds up well in the fridge, so feel free to make the dressing and toast the hazelnuts in advance, and make the salad as you want it.

Servings: 8

Ingredients

½ cup <u>chopped hazelnuts</u>

1 head iceberg lettuce

1½ cups <u>Gorgonzola Dressing</u> recipe on page 88

Instructions

- You'll want to have your dressing made and waiting.

- Spread your hazelnuts on a rimmed baking sheet, and give them 6-7 minutes at 350° F. If you roast them pre-chopping, you can then roll them between your palms and the brown skin will flake off, but this is hardly essential. Do chop them fairly coarsely, so they contribute good texture.

- Cut wedges from a head of iceberg lettuce, ⅛ head is one serving. Top each with 3 tablespoons dressing and a tablespoon of chopped hazelnuts. That's it!

Nutritionals
Per Serving: 209 Calories; 21g Fat (86.8% calories from fat); 4g Protein; 4g Carbohydrate; 2g Dietary Fiber; 17mg Cholesterol; 188mg Sodium.

Time Machine Chicken Salad

By Dana Carpender

This started with a recipe called "Chicken Mayonnaise" from a cookbook written in 1960. It sounded like an oddly flavored mayonnaise, but then I realized it was fancy-speak for "Chicken with Lots of Mayonnaise." The egg and capers were thrown in as garnish, but I turned them into actual ingredients, and I changed the proportions a bit. I also added the shirataki to bulk it up. I really liked this; once again, recipes from the days before fat-phobia turn out to be our friends.

Servings: 6

Ingredients

1 packet tofu shirataki, <u>macaroni</u> shape

¼ cup <u>chopped walnuts</u>

1 cup diced chicken

1 hard-boiled egg, peeled and chopped

1½ teaspoons capers

½ cup mayonnaise or <u>Fat Fast Ketonnaise</u> recipe on page 82

½ teaspoon <u>Tabasco sauce</u>, or <u>Frank's Hot Sauce</u>

Salt and pepper

Instructions

- Prepare your shirataki as described in the <u>Preparing Shirataki Noodles</u> section on pages 35 & 36.

- Preheat oven to 325° F. Spread the walnuts in a shallow baking tin, slide them in, and give them about 7-8 minutes. (Set the timer!)

- In the meanwhile, dice your chicken and peel and chop your egg. Throw 'em in a mixing bowl. Drain the capers and chop them, too, before adding them.

- By now the oven timer has beeped. Pull out your walnuts and chop them up. Add them to the mix.

- We'll assume the shirataki is ready now. Add to the bowl.

- Now stir in the mayonnaise and Tabasco. Salt and pepper to taste, and it's done. Chilling it before serving is nice, but not essential.

Nutritionals
Per Serving: 257 Calories; 25g Fat (84.6% calories from fat); 10g Protein; 1g Carbohydrate; trace Dietary Fiber; 70mg Cholesterol; 149mg Sodium.

Sun-Dried Tomato and Pesto Stuffed Mushrooms

By Dana Carpender

I confess, the combination of the red tomatoes and the green pesto makes the stuffing here kind of brownish. But they're very easy, and super-tasty.

Servings: 5

Ingredients

8 ounces mushrooms

3 tablespoons olive oil

4 ounces cream cheese, softened

1 tablespoon sun-dried tomatoes, oil-packed

1 tablespoon pesto sauce

Instructions

- Preheat oven to 350° F.

- Wipe your mushrooms with a damp paper towel. Remove the stems and reserve for some other purpose, like slicing and sautéing to eat for another Fat Fast feeding.

- Put the olive oil in an 8"x 8" pan. Put in the mushroom caps, turn them over and over, coating them with the oil. Let them sit and absorb oil while you...

- Put the cream cheese, sun-dried tomatoes, and pesto in the food processor. Pulse, scraping down the sides of the bowl once or twice, until it's all evenly mixed.

- Stuff the cream cheese mixture into the mushrooms, and bake for 40 minutes. Eat hot, they rewarm nicely. I got about 5 mushrooms per serving, but then my mushroom caps were small. I'm trusting you can count your mushrooms and divide by 5.

Nutritionals

Per Serving: 180 Calories; 18g Fat (86.3% calories from fat); 3g Protein; 3g Carbohydrate; 1g Dietary Fiber; 26mg Cholesterol; 93mg Sodium.

Chocolate Milk

By Dana Carpender

Does anyone really outgrow chocolate milk? Microwave for cocoa. By the way, look at that fiber count, cocoa powder is full of the stuff!

Servings: 1

Ingredients

½ cup full-fat canned coconut milk, unsweetened

¾ cup water

36 drops vanilla liquid stevia

1 tablespoon unsweetened cocoa powder

Instructions

- Just put everything in your blender and run it for 30 seconds or so. That's it!

Nutritionals

Per Serving: 234 Calories; 24g Fat (85.7% calories from fat); 3g Protein; 6g Carbohydrate; 2g Dietary Fiber; 0mg Cholesterol; 29mg Sodium.

Notes

If you prefer, you can use liquid sucralose to equal 2 tablespoons of sugar in sweetness, plus ¼ teaspoon vanilla extract, to replace the stevia.

Morning Mocha

By Dana Carpender

Great on a hot summer morning. Feel free to microwave it in the winter for a hot beverage, too. Either way, it'll get you out of the house fast.

Servings: 1

Ingredients

½ cup full-fat canned coconut milk, unsweetened

1 cup water

2 teaspoons unsweetened cocoa powder

1 teaspoon instant coffee

1 tablespoon sugar free caramel coffee syrup

1 tablespoon sugar free chocolate coffee syrup

Instructions

- Simple! Just assemble everything in your blender or a jar with a tight lid.
- Blend or shake until the coffee and cocoa are completely blended in, pour, and drink.

Nutritionals

Per Serving: 230 Calories; 24g Fat (87.4% calories from fat); 3g Protein; 5g Carbohydrate; 1g Dietary Fiber; 0mg Cholesterol; 30mg Sodium.

Notes

I bought a carton of So Delicious brand unsweetened coconut milk in the carton, the kind meant for drinking or pouring on cereal (yeah, right). Sadly, the stuff is so watery it makes skim milk seem like half-and-half. Most of the few calories it has do come from fat, but you'd have to drink a quart to get a single feeding, and I can't imagine why you would. However, I did use some of it up thinning good, rich canned coconut milk, in place of plain water. Works well, and doesn't skew the fat percentage. Still, I can't see why you'd buy it just for that.

Spaghetti with Bacon and Olives

By Dana Carpender

Not only is this tasty, the brown bacon and green-and-red olives make it pretty, too. This would make a great side dish when you're not Fat Fasting, and I'm betting your family will like it, too.

Servings: 1

Ingredients

1 packet tofu shirataki, <u>spaghetti</u> shape

2 slices bacon

8 green pimento-stuffed olives

1 teaspoon minced parsley

2 teaspoons olive oil

2 teaspoons chicken broth

1 teaspoon grated Parmesan cheese

Instructions

- Prepare your shirataki as described in the <u>Preparing Shirataki Noodles</u> section on pages 35 & 36.

- In the meanwhile, use your kitchen shears to snip the bacon into a medium-sized skillet over medium heat.

- May as well chop your olives now. Or you could just buy a jar of "salad olives," sliced stuffed olives, and measure out perhaps 1½ tablespoons of them. I happened to have stuffed olives in the fridge, waiting to be used up. Go ahead and mince your parsley, too.

- Go stir your bacon!

- When the bacon bits are crispy, scoop them out with a slotted spoon and put 'em on a little plate.

- Add the olives, olive oil, and chicken broth to the grease in the skillet. Stir it all around until the nice brown stuff on the bottom of the skillet is dissolved. Turn off the burner.

- Okay, you've drained your shirataki for the final time. Add the bacon, and everything from the skillet, using a rubber scraper to get all the grease.

- Toss the shirataki, bacon, and olives together. Top with the parsley and Parmesan.

Nutritionals
Per Serving: 203 Calories; 19g Fat (85.5% calories from fat); 5g Protein; 2g Carbohydrate; 1g Dietary Fiber; 12mg Cholesterol; 573mg Sodium.

Crimini Bisque

By Dana Carpender

Forget that gluey canned mushroom soup. This is heaven. I'd pay big bucks for this at a fancy restaurant!

Servings: 6   Yield: 4½ cups

Ingredients

8 ounces crimini mushrooms, sliced

¼ cup minced onion

¼ cup butter

1 can full-fat canned coconut milk, unsweetened

¼ teaspoon glucomannan powder, guar gum, or xanthan gum, optional, sprinkled in to desired thickness as described in our Thickeners section page 42.

2 cups chicken broth

1 teaspoon chicken bouillon concentrate

½ teaspoon salt, or Vege-Sal, or to taste

½ teaspoon pepper

1 tablespoon dry sherry, optional

Instructions

- In a big, heavy saucepan, over medium-low heat, sauté the mushrooms and onion in the butter. I like to break up my mushroom slices—I buy 'em sliced—a bit more with the edge of my spatula, but admit the slices are more picturesque.

- When the mushrooms and onion are soft and have exuded liquid, transfer half of them into your blender. Add the coconut milk and the guar gum or xanthan gum, and run until the vegetables are finely pureed. Pour back into the pan with the rest of the mushrooms and onions.

- Stir in the chicken broth, chicken bouillon concentrate, salt and pepper, and sherry if using.

- Turn the burner to low, and let the whole thing cook at a little below a simmer for 10-12 minutes.

Nutritionals

Per Serving: 221 Calories; 22g Fat (85.4% calories from fat); 4g Protein; 4g Carbohydrate; 1g Dietary Fiber; 21mg Cholesterol; 587mg Sodium.

Notes

You can use regular button mushrooms if you like, but the crimini lend a great depth of flavor. Feel free to serve this over shirataki if you like.

Chicken-Olive-Almond Salad

By Dana Carpender

I had leftover Olive-Almond Spaghetti Sauce and leftover chicken kicking around the fridge, so this is what I did with them. Servings are quite small, as you can see, but it's mighty tasty.

Servings: 5

Ingredients

1 package Miracle Rice

½ cup diced chicken

⅔ cup Olive-Almond Spaghetti Sauce recipe on page 95

1 tablespoon mayonnaise or Fat Fast Ketonnaise recipe on page 82

2 tablespoons crumbled feta cheese

Instructions

- Prepare the Miracle Rice as described in the Preparing Shirataki Noodles section on pages 35 & 36.

- When the Miracle Rice has cooled to room temperature, stir in everything else. Done.

Nutritionals

Per Serving: 233 Calories; 23g Fat (84.7% calories from fat); 6g Protein; 3g Carbohydrate; 1g Dietary Fiber; 21mg Cholesterol; 128mg Sodium.

Recipes 88% Fat and Up

Here you will find the super-high-fat recipes—88% of calories or more from fat. The more you choose from this chapter, the deeper into ketosis you're likely to go. Too, these recipes will help balance out the lower fat recipes in the earlier chapters. But remember: Fat Fasting is about super-high-fat *and* calorie restriction, both, so watch your portions.

88% and Up

Fat Fast Ketonnaise

By Dana Carpender

I keep changing up my mayonnaise recipe; this is the one I'm making most often these days. It's very rich, and has a good, full flavor. And because it uses MCT oil, it's highly ketogenic.

Servings: About 14

Ingredients

1 egg

2 egg yolks

1 tablespoon red wine vinegar

1 tablespoon lemon juice

1 teaspoon dry mustard

¼ teaspoon salt

1 drop liquid sucralose

1 cup MCT oil

½ cup extra virgin olive oil

Instructions

- Put everything but the oil in your blender. Start it running while you measure both oils into a measuring cup with a pouring lip.
- Now, with the blender running constantly, start pouring in the oil slowly, in a stream the diameter of a pencil lead.

- Your mayonnaise will reach a point where the oil starts puddling on the surface. Turn the blender to its highest speed, and use a rubber scraper to mess it around on the surface just enough that the oil gets sucked down into the blades. You should be able to work in all the oil.

- Scrape into a jar, lid tightly, and refrigerate. I can take as long as two weeks to use this up, and have had no problems.

Nutritionals
Per Serving: 220 Calories; 24g Fat (98.1% calories from fat); 1g Protein; trace Carbohydrate; trace Dietary Fiber; 44mg Cholesterol; 43mg Sodium.

Notes
If you have your own favorite mayonnaise recipe, feel free to make it using MCT oil to get a more ketogenic mayonnaise.

If you have a stick blender, and a jar with a mouth big enough to accommodate it, feel free to make this mayo right in the jar. I have a nice glass mayonnaise jar that I really like, it goes through the dishwasher like a champ, but it doesn't fit my stick blender. You can also do this in your food processor.

If you're nervous about raw eggs, look for pasteurized eggs. But be aware that the risk of a properly refrigerated, uncracked egg being contaminated with salmonella was estimated at 1 in 25,000 back in the 1990s, and the risk has been dropping since. I've never gotten sick from homemade mayo.

Ranch Dip

By Dana Carpender

Super-simple, and so much better—and better for you—than the bottled stuff, at least if you use <u>Fat Fast Ketonnaise</u> to make it! Scoop this with a few cucumber slices or celery sticks.

Servings: 5   Yield: 1 cup

Ingredients

½ cup mayonnaise or <u>Fat Fast Ketonnaise</u> recipe on page 82

½ cup sour cream

1 teaspoon minced parsley

¼ teaspoon pepper

¼ teaspoon salt

½ clove garlic, crushed

2 teaspoons minced onion

¼ teaspoon dried thyme

¼ teaspoon dried dill weed

Instructions

- Just assemble everything in your food processor with the S-blade in place, and run, scraping down the sides once or twice, until it's all well-blended and the onion and parsley are even more finely minced.

- Put it in a snap-top container and stash in the fridge. It's good right away, but improves overnight as the flavors marry.

Nutritionals
Per Serving: 208 Calories; 24g Fat (95.8% calories from fat); 1g Protein; 1g Carbohydrate; trace Dietary Fiber; 18mg Cholesterol; 244mg Sodium.

88% and Up

Caesar Dressing

By Dana Carpender

Bottled Caesar dressing is so often harsh, but this is rich and mellow. I used two anchovies, because I only like a hint of them, but my husband, an anchovy fiend, said he'd love it with another anchovy or two.

Servings: 6   Yield: 1 cup

Ingredients

2 anchovy fillets, or up to 4, to taste

2 tablespoons Dijon mustard, or spicy brown

1 tablespoon white balsamic vinegar, white

2 tablespoons Worcestershire sauce

2 cloves garlic, peeled and crushed

1 tablespoon lemon juice

1 egg

½ cup extra virgin olive oil

¼ cup grated Parmesan cheese

Instructions

- Assemble everything from the anchovies through the egg in your food processor, with the S-blade in place. Run for a minute or so, until the anchovies are pulverized. While that's happening, measure your olive oil into a measuring cup with a pouring lip.

- Now, with the processor running, slowly pour in the oil in a stream about the diameter of a pencil lead. Your dressing should emulsify.

- Add the Parmesan cheese and pulse to mix it in. That's it. Store in a tightly-lidded container in the fridge, and use it up within a few days, because of that egg.

Nutritionals
198 Calories; 20g Fat
(89.6% calories from fat); 3g Protein;
2g Carbohydrate; trace Dietary Fiber;
35mg Cholesterol; 232mg Sodium.

Asparagus with Browned Butter

By Dana Carpender

Servings: 1

This is the sort of thing you would make for company, yet it's quick and easy. Feel free to quadruple it, using a whole pound of asparagus and a whole stick of butter, and serve it to any lucky folks who might be hanging around. No less an authority than Miss Manners assures me that it is polite to eat asparagus with your fingers, so long as you can avoid getting them messy. So pour your butter over all but the bottom inch of your asparagus.

Ingredients

4 ounces asparagus

2 tablespoons butter

1 teaspoon minced shallot

Instructions

- Snap the ends off of your asparagus where they want to break naturally. Steam the rest just until brilliantly green—if it's limp, you overcooked it. I give mine 2-3 minutes in my microwave steamer. Uncover it the second it's done, or it will continue to steam and be ruined!

- In the meanwhile, melt the butter over medium-low heat. Let it cook alone for a minute or two, then add the minced shallot, and sauté until it's limp and the butter in nicely browned.

- Obviously, serve the butter and shallot over the asparagus. Lick any residual butter off the plate; it's part of your fat count!

Nutritionals
Per Serving: 219 Calories; 23g Fat (91.3% calories from fat); 2g Protein; 3g Carbohydrate; 1g Dietary Fiber; 62mg Cholesterol; 236mg Sodium.

88% and Up

Vichyssoise

By Dana Carpender

I admit, this makes a lot of servings. It's just that you need that leek, you see, and I didn't want to leave you with half-a-leek leftover. So share, or freeze this in serving-sized containers.

Servings: 12

Ingredients

1 small leek

¼ cup butter

9 ounces cauliflower

4 cups chicken broth

3 cups heavy cream

Glucomannan powder, guar gum, or xanthan gum, sprinkled in to desired thickness as described in our Thickeners section on page 42

Salt and pepper, to taste

Instructions

- Cut the green leaves and the roots off the white part of your leek. Split the white part down the middle, and rinse between the layers—leeks can hold bits of grit. Mince the leek.

- In a large, heavy bottomed saucepan, melt the butter over medium-low heat. Sauté the leek until soft.

- While the leek is softening, break or cut your cauliflower into small chunks.

- When the leek is soft, add the cauliflower and chicken broth. Turn up the heat and bring the broth to a boil, then immediately turn down to a bare simmer. Let it cook until the cauliflower is soft, probably 30 minutes, depending on how small your cauliflower bits are.

- Let your soup cool. Use your stick blender to puree the cauliflower and leek. Blend in the cream.

- Thicken a touch using your guar gum or xanthan gum shaker if you think it needs it. Salt and pepper to taste.

- Traditional vichyssoise is served chilled, with a few chives snipped on top. But if you like it better hot, who am I to argue?

Nutritionals
Per Serving: 262 Calories; 26g Fat (88.7% calories from fat); 3g Protein; 4g Carbohydrate; 1g Dietary Fiber; 92mg Cholesterol; 324mg Sodium.

Creamy Lemon Noodles

By Dana Carpender

These noodles are unusual, with a bright lemon flavor to their creamy sauce. A snap to make, too. If you wanted to take the trouble, a teaspoon of minced parsley would look pretty and taste good, but it's hardly essential.

Servings: 1

Ingredients

1 package tofu shirataki,
    fettuccini or spaghetti shape

1 ounce cream cheese, cut in 1" cubes

1 tablespoon butter

2 teaspoons lemon juice

⅛ teaspoon lemon zest

½ small garlic clove, crushed

Salt and pepper, to taste

Instructions

- Prepare your shirataki as described in the Preparing Shirataki Noodles section on pages 35 & 36.

- When the noodles have had their final draining, add the cream cheese, butter, lemon juice, lemon zest, and garlic. Toss madly with two forks until everything is melted together into a smooth sauce.

- Salt and pepper to taste. That's it!

Nutritionals
Per Serving: 206 Calories; 21g Fat (91.3% calories from fat); 2g Protein; 2g Carbohydrate; trace Dietary Fiber; 62mg Cholesterol; 201mg Sodium.

Gorgonzola Dressing

By Dana Carpender

I came up with this for the <u>Iceberg Wedge with Gorgonzola Dressing and Hazelnuts</u>, but quickly realized it had broader applications. Dip with celery sticks or cucumber slices for a super-simple "feeding."

Serving Size ¼ cup   Servings: 6   Yield: 1½ cups

Ingredients

½ cup sour cream

½ cup mayonnaise or <u>Fat Fast Ketonnaise</u>
   recipe on page 82

½ cup crumbled gorgonzola cheese

1 tablespoon lemon juice

¼ teaspoon pepper

2 dashes <u>Tabasco sauce</u>

Instructions

- Just whisk everything together.
- Store in a snap-top container or lidded jar in the fridge; it improves overnight as the flavors blend.

Nutritionals
Per Serving: 207 Calories; 22g Fat (92.2% calories from fat); 3g Protein; 1g Carbohydrate; trace Dietary Fiber; 23mg Cholesterol; 242mg Sodium.

Lime Vanilla Fat Bombs

By Dana Carpender

These were actually a mistake, I meant to make Pina colada fat bombs, but grabbed the vanilla syrup instead of the pineapple. So I added lime juice and zest, and they worked out nicely.

Servings: 16

Ingredients

2 cups shredded coconut meat

1 cup coconut oil

⅓ cup vanilla sugar-free coffee flavoring syrup

2 tablespoons lime juice

¼ teaspoon grated lime zest

1 teaspoon vanilla extract

Instructions

- Put the coconut in your food processor, and run it until you have coconut butter, at least 12-15 minutes. You'll need to scrape down the sides of the food processor a few times during this process.

- Add everything else, and run the food processor until everything is well-blended.

- Dump the mixture into an 8"x 8" pan, and press out into an even layer. Stick 'er in the fridge.

- When it's half-chilled, score into sixteen 2"x 2" bars, then refrigerate the rest of the way. Store in the fridge.

Nutritionals
Per Serving: 154 Calories; 17g Fat (94.8% calories from fat); trace Protein; 2g Carbohydrate; 1g Dietary Fiber; 0mg Cholesterol; 2mg Sodium.

Salted Caramel Mocha Keto Coffee

By Dana Carpender

Not only will this keep you satisfied and running on all cylinders for hours, but just think of the money you'll save skipping that morning latte stop!

Servings: 1

Ingredients

1 tablespoon unsalted butter, grass-fed

1 tablespoon coconut oil

1 tablespoon unsweetened cocoa powder

1 tablespoon caramel sugar-free coffee syrup

1 pinch salt, tiny pinch

1 cup brewed coffee

Instructions

- Easy! Just assemble everything in your blender, and run until it's creamy and frothy.

- Pour and drink, though I generally give mine 30 seconds in the microwave before drinking, because blending cools it a bit.

Nutritionals
Per Serving: 236 Calories; 26g Fat (91.7% calories from fat); 1g Protein; 4g Carbohydrate; 2g Dietary Fiber; 31mg Cholesterol; 141mg Sodium.

Spaghetti with Garlic & Mushrooms

By Dana Carpender

See that half-clove of garlic? No reason not to double this so you can use a whole clove. Just refrigerate the second portion, and nuke a second packet of shirataki for another feeding.

Servings: 1

Ingredients

1 package tofu shirataki, <u>spaghetti</u> shape

1 ounce sliced mushrooms, about 2 medium mushrooms

1 tablespoon butter

2 teaspoons extra virgin olive oil

½ clove garlic, crushed

1½ tablespoons grated Parmesan cheese

1 teaspoon minced parsley

Instructions

- Prepare your shirataki as described in the <u>Preparing Shirataki Noodles</u> section on pages 35 & 36.

- In the meanwhile, start the mushrooms sautéing in the butter and olive oil, over medium heat. I like to break them up a little more as they sauté, but do as you please.

- When the mushrooms have softened and changed color, stir in the garlic. Let it sauté just another minute.

- Noodles done nuking and draining? Dump the mushrooms on top and toss. Top with the Parmesan and parsley, and yum it down.

Nutritionals

Per Serving: 225 Calories; 23g Fat (89.3% calories from fat); 4g Protein; 2g Carbohydrate; trace Dietary Fiber; 37mg Cholesterol; 259mg Sodium.

88% and Up

Celery Salad

By Dana Carpender

Clearly, this is for celery lovers. It helps to have a food processor with a thin-slicing blade, or you'll be in for some cutting board work. Still, nice on a hot summer day. This, by the way, is a great example of how celery really is diet food.

Servings: 5

Ingredients

1 bunch celery

½ cup olive oil

3 tablespoons red wine vinegar

1 teaspoon tarragon

1 teaspoon salt

½ teaspoon pepper

2 tablespoons brown mustard

1 teaspoon dry mustard

Instructions

- Simple! Slice the celery crosswise as thinly as you can, and plunk it in a mixing bowl. Put everything else in a clean jar, screw the lid on tightly, and shake hard. Pour it over the celery and stir it all up. Refrigerate for at least an hour or two, then stir again before serving.

Nutritionals

Per Serving: 202 Calories; 22g Fat (95.6% calories from fat); 1g Protein; 2g Carbohydrate; trace Dietary Fiber; 0mg Cholesterol; 515mg Sodium.

Quasi-Mexican Mocha

By Dana Carpender

The combination of chocolate, vanilla, and cinnamon is quintessentially Mexican. The English toffee stevia is less so, but stands in here for pilloncillo, traditional Mexican brown sugar.

Servings: 1

Ingredients

¼ cup heavy cream, chilled

12 drops English toffee liquid stevia

1 cup brewed coffee, strong

1 teaspoon cocoa powder

1 pinch cinnamon

2 drops orange liquid stevia

18 drops vanilla liquid stevia

Instructions

- First, whip the cream with the English toffee stevia, using an electric mixer or a whisk. You want it so it mounds beautifully, but isn't stiff.

- Put everything else in the blender, and run it for just a minute. Pour into a cup. If it's cooled a bit too much, you can nuke it for 30 seconds at this point.

- Top with the whipped cream, and indulge.

Nutritionals
Per Serving: 214 Calories; 22g Fat (90.1% calories from fat); 2g Protein; 4g Carbohydrate; 1g Dietary Fiber; 82mg Cholesterol; 28mg Sodium.

Notes
You do realize you can quadruple the whipped cream, using a full half-pint carton, and have it ready to go in the fridge, right? It'll keep a day or so.

Dutch Artichoke and "Rice" Salad

By Dana Carpender

An adaptation from a James Beard cookbook written before fat phobia hit, this is rich and delicious.

Servings: 8

Ingredients

2 packages <u>Miracle Rice</u>

14 ounces canned artichoke hearts, drained and chopped

2 tablespoons roasted red pepper, chopped

⅓ cup olive oil

2 tablespoons red wine vinegar

1 tablespoon lemon juice

½ teaspoon salt

¼ teaspoon pepper

¼ teaspoon paprika, sweet

½ cup mayonnaise or <u>Fat Fast Ketonnaise</u> recipe on page 84

1 tablespoon heavy cream

3 tablespoons crumbled blue cheese

2 tablespoons minced parsley

1 tablespoon dill weed, fresh

Instructions

- Prepare the Miracle Rice as described in the <u>Preparing Shirataki Noodles</u> section on pages 35 & 36.

- Drain and chop the artichoke hearts and roasted red pepper.

- Put the vinegar, lemon juice, salt, pepper, paprika, and mayonnaise in a clean old jar, lid it tightly, and shake furiously.

- When the Miracle Rice is thoroughly drained and has cooled to room temperature, throw it in a mixing bowl. Add the artichokes and pepper, then pour on the dressing and toss. Now stir in the heavy cream and crumbled blue cheese, and toss again. Store in a covered container in the fridge.

- This is good chilled, but I like it even better at room temperature. Since your serving will be about ½ cup, it shouldn't take long to warm up a bit.

Nutritionals
Per Serving: 216 Calories; 22g Fat (88.5% calories from fat); 2g Protein; 4g Carbohydrate; trace Dietary Fiber; 10mg Cholesterol; 381mg Sodium.

Olive-Almond Spaghetti Sauce

By Dana Carpender

An unusual and delicious sauce, and a snap to make assuming you have pitted green olives in the house. Make sure they're good ones, though. The whole thing hinges on the quality of those olives.

Servings: 6   Yield: 1¼ cups

Ingredients

½ cup olive oil, divided

½ cup sliced almonds

10 green olives, pitted

2 tablespoons lemon juice

2 drops orange extract

1 teaspoon dried oregano, or 1 tablespoon fresh

1 clove garlic, crushed

1 teaspoon chipotle hot sauce

Instructions

- Put a medium-sized, heavy skillet over medium low heat. Add 2 tablespoons of the oil, then the almonds. Stir until the almonds are nicely toasted. Remove from the heat!

- With the S-blade in place, put the olives in your food processor. Pulse 6-8 times. Now add everything else, including the almonds, and pulse another 4-5 times. That's it!

- What do you do with this? Toss it with shirataki spaghetti or angel hair, of course. Yum.

Nutritionals

Per Serving: 241 Calories; 25g Fat (90.3% calories from fat); 3g Protein; 3g Carbohydrate; 1g Dietary Fiber; 0mg Cholesterol; 86mg Sodium.

Notes

How do you get 6 servings from 1¼ cups (roughly) of sauce? Figure about 3 tablespoons per serving.

If your olives aren't pitted, smash each one with your thumb to loosen the pit.

88% and Up

Honey-Mustard Dressing/Dip

By Dana Carpender

This Honey-Mustard Dressing/Dip recipe is a perennial favorite, especially with chicken. I devised this to go with wings, but you could just dip it with celery or cucumber slices. In that case, though, your serving would be bigger, about 2 rounded tablespoons.

Servings: 4

Yield: 7 tablespoons

Ingredients

5 tablespoons mayonnaise or <u>Fat Fast Ketonnaise</u> recipe on page 82

5 teaspoons brown mustard

18 drops <u>English toffee liquid stevia</u>

2 drops <u>liquid sucralose</u>, or to equal 2 teaspoons sugar in sweetness

⅛ teaspoon salt, or <u>Vege-Sal</u>

½ teaspoon cider vinegar

Instructions

- This could not be simpler: Measure everything into a bowl. Stir it together. Done.

- Store in a lidded jar or snap-top container in the fridge.

- For bonus easiness points, stir it up right in the jar.

Nutritionals

Per Serving: 129 Calories; 15g Fat (96.7% calories from fat); 1g Protein; trace Carbohydrate; trace Dietary Fiber; 6mg Cholesterol; 183mg Sodium.

Tropical Cooler

By Dana Carpender

This really needs a little paper umbrella. By the way, DaVinci Gourmet makes the sugar-free pineapple syrup, and a very useful item it is, too, though I wouldn't try it in coffee.

Servings: 1

Ingredients

½ cup <u>full-fat canned coconut milk</u>, unsweetened

1 tablespoon lemon juice

1 teaspoon lime juice

1 tablespoon <u>pineapple sugar-free syrup</u>

⅛ teaspoon orange extract

½ cup sugar-free ginger ale, chilled

Instructions

- Measure the coconut milk, lemon juice, lime juice, pineapple syrup, and orange extract into a tall glass.
- Add ice if you like, but it's not essential.
- Pour in the ginger ale, give it a gentle stir, et voila!

Nutritionals

Per Serving: 228 Calories; 24g Fat (88.3% calories from fat); 2g Protein; 5g Carbohydrate; trace Dietary Fiber; 0mg Cholesterol; 53mg Sodium.

"Tapioca" Pudding

By Dana Carpender

The first time I tried Miracle Rice I noticed it was more like tapioca than rice, and this recipe became a certainty. Rich and luscious, you'll want to hide this from the rest of the family.

Servings: 6

Ingredients

1 can full-fat canned coconut milk, unsweetened

1 package Miracle Rice

3 egg yolks

¼ teaspoon vanilla liquid stevia

¼ teaspoon English toffee liquid stevia

¼ teaspoon salt

¼ teaspoon vanilla extract

½ cup heavy cream, chilled

Instructions

- Pour the coconut milk into a 2-cup Pyrex measure with a pouring lip. Microwave it until hot through, about 3 minutes.

- Prepare the Miracle Rice as described in the Preparing Shirataki Noodles section on pages 35 & 36—nuke it after the coconut milk is good and hot.

- Put the egg yolks in a deep, narrow bowl—save the whites for another recipe, or just give 'em to the dog. Add the two flavors of stevia, the salt, and the vanilla. Whisk them together thoroughly, until very smooth. Whisk in the hot coconut milk, a little at a time.

- Pour this into the top of a double boiler, over water that is hot but not boiling. Whisk constantly until the mixture thickens—probably 5-7 minutes or so. This custard should be a little thicker than heavy cream.

- When the custard has thickened, remove it from the heat, let it cool, stir in the Miracle Rice, and chill it.

- When the custard mixture is good and cold, whip the heavy cream until stiff. Be careful not to overbeat, or you'll get butter!

- Add half of the whipped cream to the chilled custard and fold it in with a rubber scraper. Repeat with the second half of the whipped cream. Chill again before serving—if you can resist.

Nutritionals
Per Serving: 223 Calories; 23g Fat (90.0% calories from fat); 3g Protein; 3g Carbohydrate; trace Dietary Fiber; 134mg Cholesterol; 112mg Sodium.

ACKNOWLEDGEMENTS

Producing the Fat Fast Cookbook 2 was a labor of love made by an amazing team.

Dana Carpender has been one of my best friends since 1999 and continues to inspire me every day. We will continue to collaborate on more Low-Carb books/ eBooks so keep watching CarbSmart.com.

Jacqueline A. Eberstein, RN has been a friend of CarbSmart for many, many years. Although I met **Dr. Atkins** a couple of times before his untimely death, I could not say we were friends. Jacqueline was Dr. Atkins' clinical nurse for over 20 years and is the foremost authority on the Fat Fast there is. I met Jacqueline back in 1999 and enjoyed seeing her and working with her on a few CarbSmart projects over the years. She has been administering the Fat Fast to her patients for decades! She has seen first hand how the Fat Fast works to get her stalled patients back into Nutritional Ketosis.

Glendon J. Robbins (Jim) was one of the first friends I made when I moved to Las Vegas in 2013. Jim is an amazing photographer that goes out of his way to make sure we produce the best photos for our projects.

Christine Pesta was instrumental in the styling of the photographs for the recipes in this book. Thank you Christine for your time and dedication to our projects.

Amy Dungan has been a part of the CarbSmart team for a long, long time. She has written articles for CarbSmart.com, she shot the first five video recipes in the CarbSmart's Dana Carpender's Low-Carb for Life series on YouTube, photographed hundreds of recipes for us over the years, and contributed some awesome recipes to the original Fat Fast Cookbook. Although moving into other areas of publishing, Amy was able to photograph our amazing cover image (as she did in the first Fat Fast Cookbook) for this cookbook.

John Furkin is a designer and friend who goes beyond the call of duty to make sure that every project he does (especially every project he does for CarbSmart) is perfect. When I have a printing project, I contact John first.

RESOURCES

If you have any questions about the content of this cookbook or wish to report any broken links, please email **comments@carbsmart.com** immediately.

FatFastRecipes.com
—The home of the **Fat Fast Cookbook** and **Fat Fast Cookbook 2** has the largest collection of information related to the Fat Fast. Here you'll find free Fat Fast recipes, a list of ingredients for making your Fat Fast recipes, the PDF version of the first Fat Fast Cookbook, and many other resources.

Purchase Kindle version of **Fat Fast Cookbook** or **Fat Fast Cookbook 2** on Amazon.com (search Amazon.com for **Fat Fast Cookbook**).

Purchase Nook version of **Fat Fast Cookbook** or **Fat Fast Cookbook 2** on BarnesandNoble.com (search barnesandnoble.com for **Fat Fast Cookbook**).

Purchase Apple iBook version of **Fat Fast Cookbook** or **Fat Fast Cookbook 2** in Apple iBookstore (search iTunes for **Fat Fast Cookbook**).

Purchase Google Play version of **Fat Fast Cookbook** or **Fat Fast Cookbook 2** in Google Play Bookstore (search Google Play for **Fat Fast Cookbook**).

Ingredients from Fat Fast Cookbook 2
—We've made it easy for you to purchase all the ingredients you need for your Fat Fast recipes by going to *CarbSmart.com/ffc2*.

Dana Carpender's Page on Amazon.com
—We've made it easy for you to purchase all of Dana's books from *Amazon.com*.

CarbSmart.com
—CarbSmart is the publisher of **Fat Fast Cookbook** and **Fat Fast Cookbook 2**. The web site **CarbSmart.com** is your trusted guide to the low-carb lifestyle. Since 1999, we've published the latest news, information, product reviews, and success stories to help you succeed at your low-carb lifestyle. Visit us at **www.CarbSmart.com**.

GlutenSmart.com
—GlutenSmart is the sister website to CarbSmart focusing on the needs of the Celiac and gluten-free community and will soon be publishing it's own series of gluten-free cookbooks. Visit us at **www.GlutenSmart.com**.

HoldTheToast.com
—The web site of Dana Carpender, the author of **Fat Fast Cookbook** and **Fat Fast Cookbook 2**. Dana has been publishing her perspective on the low-carb lifestyle since 1999.

Amy Dungan Photography
—The (photography) web site of Amy Dungan, contributor to the **Fat Fast Cookbook 2**.

ABOUT THE AUTHORS

Dana Carpender

A pioneer of the low carb frontier, best-selling author Dana Carpender went low carb in 1995, after whole-grain-and-beaning her way up to a size 20. Immediate weight loss and sky-rocketing energy told her this was what her body had been waiting for her to do, that she had set her foot on a path from which there was no return. However, it rapidly became clear that to set this way for life, she—and others—needed the answer to one simple question: What's for dinner? The answer will be found in her cookbooks, twenty of them so far, encompassing over 2,500 recipes. Dana has been fighting the low-fat lie since 1998 at HoldTheToast.com. She lives in Indiana with three dogs, a cat, a backyard full of chickens—and, of course, That Nice Boy She Married, with whom she shares much bacon on a pleasant Sunday morning.

Andrew S. DiMino

Andrew DiMino spent most of his life sickly, overweight, and wondering if he could ever lose the excess pounds. He started a new diet every week—usually based on a low-calorie, low-fat diet—with no lasting results. All he had ever heard about were high carbohydrate, calorie counting diets that the medical profession was so fond of. But, they never worked and he usually gained more weight.

In 1998 he learned he was a type-2 diabetic and instead of eating the foods his doctor told him to eat, he read Dr. Atkins' New Diet Revolution. It changed his life. He lost 50 pounds in 4 months, controlled his diabetes and stopped worrying about calories, grams of fat, or major exercise programs that just made him hungrier. He started CarbSmart.com and sold thousands of Low-Carb and Gluten-Free products until 2012 when CarbSmart dropped all the foods and evolved into an online magazine. Now CarbSmart's mission is to help those who want to change their life with a Low-Carb lifestyle. They accomplish it by publishing the best recipes that Dana Carpender and the CarbSmart team can devise.

Low-Carb Products Listed in Fat Fast Recipes

The nature of being a low-carber means that we give up using the ingredients we've been eating most of our life—usually highly processed and packaged foods—for better, healthier ingredients. Normally that means we eat meats, fish, veggies, and dairy everyday. Some of these foods are in this book but during a Fat Fast, we have to choose other specialized ingredients.

So throughout this cookbook, you'll see ingredients listed with an underline—like full-fat canned coconut milk. When you see these underlined ingredients, go to the CarbSmart.com website for links where to find the items:

https://www.carbsmart.com/ffc2

Printed in Great Britain
by Amazon